Mastering C++
Programming Language

Mastering Computer Science
Series Editor: Sufyan bin Uzayr

Mastering C++ Programming Language: A Beginner's Guide
Divya Sachdeva and Natalya Ustukpayeva

Mastering Git: A Beginner's Guide
Sumanna Kaul, Shahryar Raz, and Divya Sachdeva

Mastering Ruby on Rails: A Beginner's Guide
Mathew Rooney and Madina Karybzhanova

Mastering Sketch: A Beginner's Guide
Mathew Rooney and Md Javed Khan

Mastering C#: A Beginner's Guide
Mohamed Musthafa MC, Divya Sachdeva, and Reza Nafim

Mastering GitHub Pages: A Beginner's Guide
Sumanna Kaul and Shahryar Raz

For more information about this series, please visit: https://www.routledge.com/Mastering-Computer-Science/book-series/MCS

The "Mastering Computer Science" series of books are authored by the Zeba Academy team members, led by Sufyan bin Uzayr.

Zeba Academy is an EdTech venture that develops courses and content for learners primarily in STEM fields, and offers education consulting to Universities and Institutions worldwide. For more info, please visit https://zeba.academy

Mastering C++ Programming Language

A Beginner's Guide

Edited by Sufyan bin Uzayr

CRC Press

Taylor & Francis Group

Boca Raton London New York

CRC Press is an imprint of the
Taylor & Francis Group, an **informa** business

First edition published 2022
by CRC Press
6000 Broken Sound Parkway NW, Suite 300, Boca Raton, FL 33487-2742

and by CRC Press
2 Park Square, Milton Park, Abingdon, Oxon, OX14 4RN

CRC Press is an imprint of Taylor & Francis Group, LLC

© 2022 Sufyan bin Uzayr

ISBN: 978-1-032-10321-1 (hbk)
ISBN: 978-1-032-10320-4 (pbk)
ISBN: 978-1-003-21476-2 (ebk)

DOI: 10.1201/9781003214762

Typeset in Minion
by KnowledgeWorks Global Ltd.

Contents

About the Editor

Sufyan bin Uzayr is a writer, coder, and entrepreneur with more than a decade of experience in the industry. He has authored several books in the past, pertaining to a diverse range of topics, ranging from History to Computers/IT.

Sufyan is the Director of Parakozm, a multinational IT company specializing in EdTech solutions. He also runs Zeba Academy, an online learning and teaching vertical with a focus on STEM fields.

Sufyan specializes in a wide variety of technologies, such as JavaScript, Dart, WordPress, Drupal, Linux, and Python. He holds multiple degrees, including ones in Management, IT, Literature, and Political Science.

Sufyan is a digital nomad, dividing his time between four countries. He has lived and taught in universities and educational institutions around the globe. Sufyan takes a keen interest in technology, politics, literature, history, and sports, and in his spare time, he enjoys teaching coding and English to young students.

Learn more at sufyanism.com.

CHAPTER 1

Introduction to C++

IN THIS CHAPTER

> Getting to know the history of C++

> Learning about uses and features

> Installation of C++

C++ is a programming language that gives programs a reasonable construction and works with code reuse, reducing improvement costs. C++ is a convenient programming language that might be utilized to make applications that sudden spike in demand for various frameworks. C++ is fun and primary language to learn. C++ was made by Danish PC researcher Bjarne at Bell Labs in 1979 as an augmentation of the C language; he looked for a quick and adaptable language tantamount to C that additionally

DOI: 10.1201/9781003214762-1

included significant level abilities for a program the executives. It was first normalized in 1998. In C++, information types are divided into three classifications: types of primitive data: These are underlying or preset information types that might be utilized to pronounce factors straight by the client. For example, int, scorch, coast, bool, etc. The whole number is a crude information type open in C++.

WHAT IS C++?

C++ is a high-level programming language developed by Bjarne Stroustrup, and C++ operates on various platforms, including Windows, Mac OS, and several UNIX variants. This C++ tutorial employs a straightforward and practical approach to conveying C++ concepts to novice to advanced computer programmers.

C++ is a MUST for understudies and working experts to become extraordinary Software Engineers. I'll go through a few of the most important advantages of learning C++:

- C++ is extremely near the equipment, so you get an opportunity to work at a low level which gives you a ton of control as far as memory the board, better execution, lastly, a vigorous programming advancement.

- C++ programming gives you an unmistakable comprehension of object-oriented programming (OOP). You will comprehend the low-level execution of polymorphism when you carry out virtual tables and virtual table pointers or dynamic sort distinguishing proof.

- C++ is one of the green programming dialects and is adored by a large number of programming designers. Assuming you are an incredible C++ software engineer, you won't ever sit without work, and all the more significantly, you will get generously compensated for your work.

- C++ is the most broadly utilized programming language in application and framework programming. So you can pick your space of interest in programming advancement.

- C++ indeed shows you the distinction between compiler, linker, and loader, various information types, stockpiling classes, variable sorts, their extensions, and so on.

- **C++'s advantages include:**

  - C++ is a highly portable language that is frequently used to create multi-device, multi-platform apps.

  - Classes, inheritance, polymorphism, data abstraction, and encapsulation are all features of C++, an OOP language.

  - The C++ function library is extensive.

  - Exception handling and function overloading are both feasible in C++ but not in C.

  - C++ is a compelling, efficient, and quick programming language. It has many applications, ranging from graphical user interfaces to gaming 3D visuals to real-time mathematical calculations.

WHICH IS MORE DIFFICULT
TO LEARN: C OR C++?

Despite their similarities, C and C++ are two distinct programming languages that should be treated as such. There are still unique use cases for both C and C++ today, some 50 years after their birth.

To decide whether you should study C or C++, think about the sort of program you intend to use your acquired skills in.

C++ Compilers Are Accessible Which You
Can Use to Incorporate and Run

- IBM C++

- Intel C++

- Microsoft Visual C++

- Prophet C++

- HP C++

USES OF C++ PROGRAMMING

As referenced previously, C++ is perhaps the most generally utilized programming dialect. It has its essence in pretty much every space of programming advancement. I will list a couple of them here:

- **Application Software Development:** C++ programming has been utilized in growing practically every one of the major Operating Systems like Windows, Mac OSX, and Linux. Aside from the working frameworks, the centerpiece of numerous programs like Mozilla Firefox and Chrome has been composed utilizing C++. C++ likewise has been used in fostering the most famous data set framework called MySQL.

- **Programming Languages Development:** C++ has been utilized broadly in growing new programming dialects like C#, Java, JavaScript, Perl, UNIX's C Shell, PHP and Python, and Verilog, and so forth.

- **Calculation Programming:** C++ is the closest companion of researchers due to its quick speed and computational efficiencies.

- **Games Development:** C++ is speedy, permitting software engineers to do procedural programming for CPU-concentrated capacities and gives more extraordinary power over equipment. It has been generally utilized in the improvement of gaming motors.

- **Inserted System:** C++ is vigorously utilized in creating Medical and Engineering Applications like programming for MRI machines, excellent quality CAD/CAM frameworks, etc.

This rundown goes on; there are different regions where programming designers cheerfully utilize C++ to give extraordinary programming. I firmly prescribe you learn C++ and contribute unique virtual products to the local area.

FEATURES OF C++

There are different provisions of C++. For example:

- Object-oriented
- Simple
- Platform dependent
- Mid-level programming language
- Structured programming language
- Rich library
- Memory management
- Powerful and fast
- Pointers
- Compiler based
- Syntax-based language

OBJECT-ORIENTED PROGRAMMING LANGUAGE

The fundamental up-degree from C to C++ is object-arranged programming. It follows ideas of oh no like polymorphism, legacy, epitome, reflection. This improves and supports simpler.

We should momentarily comprehend the ideas of item arranged programming.

- **Class:** A class is a client characterized plan or model from which items are made. It addresses the arrangement of properties or techniques that are normal to all objects of one sort.

- **Object:** It is a fundamental unit of OOP and addresses genuine substances. A C++ program makes many items which associate with summoning techniques.

- **Polymorphism:** Polymorphism alludes to the capacity of OOPs programming dialects to separate between substances with a similar name proficiently.

- **Inheritance:** Inheritance is the component wherein one class is permitted to acquire the provisions for another type.

- **Encapsulation:** Encapsulation is characterized as the wrapping up of information under a solitary unit. It is the component that ties together code and the information it controls.

- **Abstraction:** Abstraction refers to displaying only the most essential information while concealing the details. Data abstraction exposes just the crucial aspects of the data to the outside world while covering the implementation specifics.

ELEMENTS OF C++

C++ gives an organized methodology wherein you can break the issue into parts and plan the arrangement separately. It gives you a rich collection of library works that you can utilize while executing the agreement.

If you have worked with C language, moving to C++ would be an incredibly smooth progressing. The language structure is practically comparable with minute changes.

Stage Dependent

Stage subordinate language implies can execute the language wherein projects distinctly on that working framework are created and ordered. It can't run or manage it on some other operational framework.

Mid-Level Programming Language

C++ can do both low-level and undeniable level programming. This is the motivation behind why C++ is known as a mid-level programming language. When we talk about low-level programming, C++ is utilized to foster framework applications like the portion, driver, and so forth.

Organized Programming Language

In C++ programming, the code is measured with capacities, classes, and protests, and the modules are approximately coupled. The secret code is straightforward and adjusts. This makes C++ an organized programming language.

Rich Library

Designers approach heaps of in-fabricated capacities given by C++ language. This saves time and makes advancement quick. We should take a gander at a portion of the C++ header records and functionalities provided by it.

- **<iostream>**: Contains C++ standard info and yield capacities

- **<iterator>**: Contains classes for getting to information in the C++ Standard Library holders

- **<iomanip>:** Contains stream controllers that arrange surges of information

- **<algorithm>:** Contains capacities for controlling information in C++ Standard Library holders

- **<cstdlib>:** Contains work for transformations of numbers to text and tight clamp versa, memory portion, varying numbers, and different other utility capacities

- **<memory>:** Contains classes and capacities utilized by the C++ Standard Library to allot memory to the C++ Standard Library holders

- **<ctime>:** Contains work for controlling the time and date

- **<fstream>:** Contains work for capacities that perform input from records on circle and yield to documents on plate

- **<cmath>:** Contains math library capacities

Memory Management

C++ upholds dynamic memory designation. You can free the distributed memory whenever. Not just this, C++ likewise gives dynamic memory to the executives' procedures.

Incredible and Fast

C++ is a quick language as arrangement and execution time is less. Additionally, it has a wide assortment of information types, capacities, and administrators.

Pointers

Pointers are factors that store the location of another variable. Pointer focuses on the memory area of a variable. C++ upholds pointer and gives answers for loads of issues that request admittance to the memory area.

Compiler-Based Language

C++ is a compiler-based programming language. Without assemblage, can be executed no C++ program. The compiler initially orders the C++ program, and afterward, it is completed.

Syntax-Based Language

C++ is a language that consents unequivocally to sentence structure. Language-keeping rules and guidelines stringently are known as close punctuation-based language. C, C++, Java, .net are a portion of the models.

ALL YOU REQUIRE TO KNOW ABOUT OBJECT-ORIENTED PROGRAMMING IN C++

Oriented programming unquestionably surprised the programming scene when it showed up and still structures reason for programming generally. In this article, we will investigate OOP in C++.

What Is Object-Oriented Programming?

- Objects

- Classes

- Encapsulation

- Abstraction

- Polymorphism

- Inheritance

Object-Oriented Programming

The significant inspiration driving the innovation of the article situated methodology is to eliminate a portion of the blemishes experienced in the procedural method. In OOP, information is treated as an essential component in the program advancement and confines its stream around the framework. It ties information near the capacity that works on it and shields it from a coincidental adjustment from outside powers. It permits the issue to break into various elements called items and afterward assembles information and capacities around these articles. The information of an item must be gotten to by the powers related to that specific article. Nonetheless, the elements of one thing can get to the aspects of different themes whenever required.

It accentuation more on information as opposed to methodology:

- The projects are separated into objects along these lines, making them simple to work with.

- Information structures are planned so that they portray the articles.

- Capacities that work on the information of an item are set together in the information structure.

- Information is covered up and can't be gotten to by outside capacities without authorization.

- Correspondence between items can occur with the assistance of capacities.

- Adding new information and capacities has gotten superficial.

Objects

Objects are the most fundamental runtime elements in OOPs. They might address user-defined information like vectors, time and records, or anything the program needs to deal with. Programming issue is investigated based on objects and the idea of correspondence between them. Articles ought to be chosen to such an extent that they match intimately with these present reality objects. Items occupy room in the memory and have no related location. At the same time, execution objects interface by sending messages to each other. For instance, on the off chance that "Understudy" and student_rollno are two articles in a program, the Student item might make an impression on the student_rollno object mentioning its related Marks. Each piece contains code to control the information.

Classes

The whole arrangement of code of an article can be made a client characterized information type with the assistance of class objects are factors of the kind class. When we describe a class, we can make quite a few items having a place with the class. Each item can be related to the information of the type class with which they are made. In this way, a class is only an assortment of objects of the comparable sort. For instance, versatile, PC, and smartwatch are altogether individuals from the class gadgets. Classes are client characterized information types. The grammar used to make an item is very straightforward. Assuming hardware has been described as a class, the assertion gadgets PC; will make an item PC having a place with the class hardware.

Encapsulation

Encapsulation can be characterized as wrapping up information and data under a solitary unit. In OOP, encapsulation is described as restricting together the knowledge and the capacities that control them.

Consider a simple illustration of exemplification; there are various areas in a school like an understudy's part, instructors segment, accounts segment, etc. The understudy segment handles all of the understudy's exercises and tracks all the information identified with finance. Also, the educator holds every one of the instructor's connected exercises and follows every one of the imprints and execution of understudies. Presently, a circumstance may emerge when an understudy from the understudy segment needs all information about imprints and execution for reasons unknown. For this situation, he isn't permitted to get to the knowledge of the instructor's component straightforwardly. He will initially need to reach some educator in the instructor area and afterward demand him give everyone the information. This is the thing that exemplification is. Here the knowledge of the understudy's part and the instructor's segment that can control them are wrapped under a solitary name of "educators area".

Abstraction

Abstraction alludes to showing just the significant and required elements of the application and concealing the subtleties. In C++, classes can give information and capacities to the rest of the world, keeping the factors stowed away from direct access, or classes can even announce everything available to everybody, or perhaps to the types acquiring it, we can transform them according to our necessities.

This should be possible utilizing access specifiers. C++ has three access specifiers:

1. Private

2. Protected

3. Public

Polymorphism

The word polymorphism implies having many structures. We can characterize polymorphism as the capacity of a capacity or information to be shown in more than one form. An individual can have various trademarks simultaneously. A kid simultaneously is an understudy, a sibling, a child so similar individual gangs diverse conduct in multiple circumstances. This is called polymorphism.

An activity can show various practices according to the necessity in multiple occurrences. The conduct relies on the sorts of information utilized and its needs in action.

C++ upholds administrator over-burdening and capacity over-burdening:

- **Administrator Overloading:** It's the way toward making an administrator display various practices in various examples.

- **Capacity Overloading:** Function over-burdening is utilizing a solitary capacity name to perform various kinds of undertakings.

Polymorphism is broadly utilized in executing legacy. Continuing with this article on OOP in C++

Inheritance

Inheritance is the cycle by which objects of one class can procure the properties, capacities, and information of objects of another class. It follows the idea of the progressive arrangement. For instance, the bird "sparrow" is a piece of the class "flying bird", a piece of the class "bird". With the assistance of this kind of division, each determined class imparts ordinary qualities and information to the class from which it is acquired. Legacy gives the possibility of reusability. This implies adding extra components to a current class without adjusting or rolling out any improvements. This is conceivable by getting another class from the current class. The new class will obtain the consolidated provisions of both parent and kid classes.

The genuine utilization of the legacy is that it permits the developer to reuse a class that is nearly, however not, what he needs, and to modify the class and make changes to not bring any unwanted incidental effects into the remainder of the classes. Note that each sub-class characterizes just those interesting provisions and its rest from its parent class. Without the utilization of any arrangement, each class would need to expressly incorporate the entirety of its elements which would have required some investment and exertion.

C++ INSTALLATION

Create and Execute a C++ Console Application Project

- You've inserted your code into a C++ console app project. You may now create and execute it directly from Visual Studio. Then, from the command line, launch it as a standalone app.

Prerequisites

- Install and run Visual Studio with the Desktop development with C++ workload on your PC. Follow the procedures in Install C++ support in Visual Studio if it isn't already installed.

Installation of Visual Studio:

- **Step 1:** Ensure that your machine is capable of running Visual Studio.
- **Step 2:** Visual Studio is available for download. Click this Link: https://visualstudio.microsoft.com/downloads/?utm_medium=microsoft&utm_source=docs.microsoft.com&utm_campaign=button+cta&utm_content=download+vs2019+rc
- **Step 3:** Install the Visual Studio setup program.
- Enter the source code for the "Hello, World!" project. Follow the instructions in Create a C++ console app project if you haven't already.

This chapter explains what C++ is and how it has evolved. What are the features, and what are the different types of compilers. Learn about C++'s purposes and features, as well as how to install C++ on your computer.

CHAPTER 2

Getting Started
With C++

IN THIS CHAPTER

> Basic syntax

> How files are handled in C++

> File handling

In the previous chapter, we covered what C++ is, its history, what it does, and what different types of compilers are and learned about C++'s uses and features and how to install C++ on a computer.

When we consider a C++ program, it tends to be characterized as an assortment of articles that convey utilizing conjuring each other's strategies. Let us currently momentarily investigate what a class, article, strategies, and moment factors mean.

DOI: 10.1201/9781003214762-2

- **Object:** Objects have states and practices; for example, A canine has states—color, name, breed just as practices—swaying, yapping, eating. An item is an example of a class.

- **Class:** A class can be characterized as a layout/plan that portrays the practices/expresses that object of its sort support.

- **Methods:** A technique is essentially conducted. A class can contain numerous strategies. It is in scenarios where the rationales are composed, information is controlled, and every one of the activities is executed.

- **Instance Variables:** Each article has its special arrangement of example factors. An article's state is made by the qualities allocated to these occasion factors.

Example:

```
#include <iostream>
using namespace std;
// main() is where program execution
begins.
int main() {
    cout << "Hello"; // prints Hello
    return 0;
}
```

COMPILE AND EXECUTE C++ PROGRAM

How about we see how to save the document, gather and run the program. Kindly follow the means given below.

Open an editor and add the code as above.

As an example, save the record .cpp

In a command window, navigate to the directory where you saved the document.

Type 'g++ example.cpp' and press enter to arrange your code. If your code is error-free, the order brief will take you to the next line and generate an executable record called a.out.

Presently type 'a.out' to run your program.

You will want to see 'Hello' imprinted on the window.

Syntax:

```
$ g++ example.cpp
$ ./a.out
Hello
```

Make sure you have g++ on your path and that you're running it in the same directory as example .cpp

SEMICOLONS AND BLOCKS

In C++, the semicolon is an assertion eliminator. That is, every individual assertion should be finished with a semicolon. It demonstrates the finish of one sensible substance.

For instance

```
a = b;
b = b + 1;
add(a, b);
```

A block is a collection of logically related sentences enclosed in opening and closing braces.

```cpp
{
   cout << "Hello"; // prints Hello
   return 0;
}
```

Identifiers

A C++ identifier is used to identify a variable, function, class, module, or any other user-defined entity. An identifier in C++ starts with a letter from A to Z, a to z, or an underscore (_), followed by zero or more letters, underscores, or numerals (0 to 9) and punctuation characters like @, $, and %. C++ is a case-sensitive programming language.

Keywords

The reserved terms in C++ are shown in the table below. These reserved terms may not be used as names for constants, variables, or other types of identifiers.

asm	else	new	this
auto	enum	operator	throw
bool	explicit	private	true
break	export	protected	try
case	extern	public	typedef
catch	false	register	typeid
char	float	reinterpret_cast	type name
class	for	return	union
const	friend	short	unsigned
const_cast	goto	signed	using
continue	if	sizeof	virtual
default	inline	static	void
delete	int	static_cast	volatile
do	long	struct	wchar_t
double	mutable	switch	while
dynamic_cast	namespace	template	

COMMENTS

Explanatory statements can be included in the C++ code as program comments. Anyone reading the source code will benefit from these remarks. All programming languages provide comments in some way.

Single-line and multi-line comments are supported in C++. The C++ compiler ignores all characters available inside each comment.

Comments in C++ begin with /* and conclude with */.

Example:

- /* This is a comment */

A comment can also start with //

- cout << "Hello World"; // prints Hello World

DATA TYPES

You must utilize numerous variables to store diverse information while developing a program in any language. Variables are just reserved memory regions where values can be stored. This implies that when you make a variable, you set aside some memory for it.

You could want to save data of different data types, such as character, wide character, integer, floating-point, double floating point, boolean, and so on. The operating allocating memory determines what can be kept in reserved memory regarding the variable's data type.

Primitive Built-In Types

C++ provides a wide range of built-in and user-defined data types to programmers. Seven fundamental C++ data types are listed in the table below.

Type	Keyword
Boolean	bool
Character	char
Integer	int
Floating point	float
Double floating point	double
Valueless	void
Wide character	wchar_t

One or more of these types of modifiers can be used to modify any of the fundamental kinds.

- signed

- unsigned

- short

- long

The table below shows the type of variable, the amount of memory needed to store the value in memory, and the highest and lowest values saved in such variables.

Type	Typical Bit Width	Typical Range
char	1 byte	−127 to 127 or 0 to 255
unsigned char	1 byte	0 to 255
signed char	1 byte	−127 to 127
int	4 bytes	−2,147,483,648 to 2,147,483,647
unsigned int	4 bytes	0 to 4,294,967,295
signed int	4 bytes	−2,147,483,648 to 2,147,483,647
short int	2 bytes	−32,768 to 32,767
unsigned short int	2 bytes	0 to 65,535
signed short int	2 bytes	−32,768 to 32,767

(Continued)

Type	Typical Bit Width	Typical Range
long int	8 bytes	–2,147,483,648 to 2,147,483,647
signed long int	8 bytes	same as long int
unsigned long int	8 bytes	0 to 4,294,967,295
long long int	8 bytes	– (2^63) to (2^63)-1
unsigned long long int	8 bytes	0 to 18,446,744,073,709,551,615
float	4 bytes	
double	8 bytes	
long double	12 bytes	
wchar_t	2 or 4 bytes	One wide character

Example:

```
#include <iostream>
using namespace std;

int main() {
    cout << "The Size of char: " <<
sizeof(char) << endl;
    cout << "The Size of int: " <<
sizeof(int) << endl;
    cout << "The Size of short int: " <<
sizeof(short int) << endl;
    return 0;
}
```

Output:

```
The Size of char: 1
The Size of int: 4
The size of short int: 2
```

VARIABLE TYPES

A variable is a kind of named stockpiling that our projects might get to. In C++, every factor has a sort that determines the memory size and format, the scope of qualities that might be put away inside that memory, and the arrangement of tasks that can be applied to the variable.

Letters, numbers, and the highlight character would all be able to be utilized in a variable's name. Either a letter or a highlight should be utilized as the primary person. Since C++ is case-delicate, upper and lowercase characters are unique.

Sr. No	Description and Type
1	**bool** True or false is stored in this variable.
2	**char** A single octet is usually used (one byte). This is a type that is made up of integers.
3	**int** The machine's most natural size of integer.
4	**float** A floating-point value with single precision.
5	**double** A floating-point value with double precision.
6	**void** The absence of type is represented by this symbol.
7	**wchar_t** A type with a large number of characters.

VARIABLE DECLARATION

A variable announcement guarantees the compiler that there is just a single variable of the predefined type and name, permitting the compiler to keep gathering without knowing the entirety of the variable's subtleties. A variable statement possibly has significance when the program is incorporated; the compiler requires a simple variable definition when the program is connected.

When utilizing a few documents, a variable assertion is helpful because you might announce your variable in one of the records that will be accessible when the application is connected. You might pronounce a variable anyplace by utilizing the extern watchword.

Example:

```
#include <iostream>
using namespace std;

// Variable declaration:
extern int x, y;
extern int z;
extern float a;

int main () {
   // Variable definition:
   int x, y;
   int z;
   float a;

   // actual initialization
   x = 20;
   y = 10;
   z = x + y;

   cout << c << endl;

   return 0;
}
```

Output:

30

Lvalues and Rvalues Are Two Distinct Sorts of Qualities

In C++, there are two sorts of articulations

An lvalue is a sort of significant worth. "Lvalue" articulations are articulations that allude to a memory area. An lvalue can be found on either the left or right half of a task.

The word rvalue alludes to information esteem that is put away in memory at a particular area. A value is an articulation that can't have a worth given to it; in this manner, it can just happen on the right half of a task, not the left.

A scope is a section of the program where variables may be declared, and there are three areas where variables can be expressed in general:

1. Local variables are found within a function or a block.

2. Formal parameters are located in the specification of function parameters.

3. Global variables are variables that exist outside of all functions.

Local Variables

Local factors are factors that are characterized inside a capacity or square. They must be used by explanations that are incorporated inside that capacity or code block.

Example:

```cpp
#include <iostream>
using namespace std;

int main () {
    // Local variable declaration:
```

```
int x, y;
int z;

// actual initialization
x = 20;
y = 10;
z = x + y;

cout << c;

return 0;
}
```

Global Level Variables

Global factors are characterized toward the start of the program, outside of any capacities. The worth of the worldwide elements will stay consistent during the existence of your program.

Any capacity approaches a global variable. That is when a global variable is pronounced, it is accessible for use all through the entire program.

Example:

```
#include <iostream>
using namespace std;

// Global variable declaration:
int g;

int main () {
    // Local variable declaration:
    int x, y;
```

```
// actual initialization
x = 20;
y = 10;
z = x + y;

cout << a;

return 0;
}
```

Initializing Local and Global Variables

When you declare a local variable, the system does not automatically initialize it; you must do it yourself. When you declare global variables like follows, the system will automatically initialize them:

Data Type	Initializer
int	0
char	'\0'
float	0
double	0
pointer	NULL

CONSTANTS

Constants, often known as literals, are fixed values that the program cannot change.

Constants are split into Integer Numerals, Floating-Point Numerals, Characters, Strings, and Boolean Values and can be of any fundamental data kinds.

- **Integer Literals:** A whole number strict is a decimal, octal, or hexadecimal steady. A prefix determines the basis or radix of a number: 0x or 0X for hexadecimal, 0 for octal, and none for decimal.

  A number exacting can be given a suffix that is a combination of U and L, which stands for unsigned and lengthy. It is possible to promote or promote the postfix, and it can appear in any grouping.

Example:

- 212   // Legal
- 215u   // Legal
- 0xFeeL   // Legal

- **Floating-point:** A number part, a decimal point, a partial part, and a type part make up a gliding point exacting. Floating-point literals can be addressed in decimal or unique structure.

  You should incorporate the decimal point, the example, or both while addressing in decimal structure and the whole number piece, the partial part, or both while addressing in remarkable structure. e or E presents the marked example.

- 3.14159   // Legal
- .e55   // Illegal: missing integer or fraction
- 314159E-5L // Legal
- 210f   // Illegal: no decimal or exponent
- 510E   // Illegal: incomplete exponent

Boolean Literals

Boolean Literals are a sort of Boolean rationale.

There are two Boolean literals in C++, the two of which are essential for the standard jargon.

- True is addressed with a worth of valid.

- False is a worth that addresses False.

You ought not to take the worth of tangible equivalent to 1 and bogus equivalent to 0 into thought.

Literals of Characters

Single statements are utilized to exemplify character literals on the off chance that the exacting beginnings with the letter L (capitalized just), it is a comprehensive person strict (e.g. L'x') that ought to be saved in a variable of type wchar t. Something else, it's simply a restricted person strict (like 'x') that might be kept in a burn type variable.

Escape Sequence	Meaning
\\	\ character
\'	' character
\"	" character
\?	? character
\a	Alert or bell
\b	Backspace
\f	Form feed
\n	Newline
\r	Carriage return
\t	Horizontal tab
\v	Vertical tab
\ooo	Octal number of one to three digits
\xhh. . .	Hexadecimal number of one or more digits

Example:

```cpp
#include <iostream>
using namespace std;
int main() {
    cout << "Hello\tHello\n\n";
    return 0;
}
```

Output:

```
Hello    Hello
```

Literals in a String

Double quotes are utilized to typify string literals. Plain characters, get away from groupings, and all-inclusive characters are among the characters in a string similar to character literals.

String literals can be utilized to partition an extended line into various lines, and whitespace can isolate them.

Example:

```
"Hello, ABC"

"Hello, \

ABC"
```

MODIFIER

C++ permits the char, int, and double data types to have modifiers going before them. A modifier is utilized to adjust the importance of the base sort to ensure that it all the more definitively fits the requirements of different circumstances.

The information type modifiers are recorded here

- signed

- unsigned

- long

- short

The modifiers marked, unsigned, long, and short can be applied to whole number base sorts. Furthermore, kept and unsigned can be applied to roast, and long can be applied to double.

The modifiers marked and unsigned can likewise be utilized as the prefix to long or short modifiers.

C++ permits shorthand documentation for proclaiming unsigned, short, or whole long numbers. You can just utilize the word unsigned, short, or long, without int. It consequently suggests int. For instance, the accompanying two assertions both pronounce unsigned number factors.

Qualifiers Types

Sr. No	Qualifier & Meaning
1	**const** Objects of type const cannot be changed while your application is running.
2	**volatile** The modifier volatile informs the compiler that a variable's value can be altered in ways not explicitly indicated in the program.
3	**restrict** Initially, a pointer qualified by restricting is the only way to access the object it references to. Only C99 introduces the determined type qualifier.

STORAGE CLASSES

In a C++ application, a storage class specifies the scope and lifespan of variables and functions. These specifiers come before the type they're changing, and they're put before the type they're changing. The storage classes mentioned here can be utilized in C++ applications.

- **auto:** For all local variables, the auto storage class is the default storage class.

  Example:

  ```
  {
     int x;
     auto int month;
  }
  ```

- **register:** The register storage class is used to create local variables that should be kept in a register rather than RAM. The variable's maximum length is equal to the register size; therefore it can't be used with the unary '&' operator.

  Example:

  ```
  {
     register int m;
  }
  ```

- **static:** The static storage class tells the compiler to keep a local variable alive for the duration of the program instead of creating and deleting it every time it enters and exits scope. As a result of making local variables static, their values are preserved between function calls.

Example:

```
static int count = 5;
```

- **extern:** The extern storage class is utilized to give a reference to a worldwide variable that is shared by all application documents. At the point when you use "extern", the variable can't be initialized since everything it does is allude the variable name to a formerly determined capacity address.

  At the point when you have a few documents and you pronounce a worldwide variable or capacity that will be utilized in different records also, you'll use extern to offer a reference to the predefined variable or capacity in another form. Just said, extern is utilized in one more code to characterize a worldwide variable or ability.

Example:

```
extern int c;
```

- **mutable:** The Modifiable Storage Class is a kind of capacity that can be changed.

  Just class objects are influenced by the impermanent specifier, which will be tended to later in this exercise. It permits an item part to supersede the const part member. That is, a const member capacity can alter a mutable part.

OPERATORS

A symbol that instructs the compiler to do certain mathematical or logical operations is known as an operator. C++ has a large number of built-in operators, including the following:

- Arithmetic Operators

- Relational Operators

- Logical Operators

- Bitwise Operators

- Assignment Operators

- Misc Operators

Arithmetic Operators

Operator	Description	Example
+	Adds two operands	C + D
−	Subtracts second operand from the first	C - D
*	Multiplies both operands	C * D
/	Divides numerator by de-numerator	D / C
%	Modulus Operator and the remainder of after an integer division	D % C
++	Increment operator increases integer value by one	C++
--	Decrement operator decreases integer value by one	C--

Relational Operators

Operator	Description	Example
==	Condition is set to true if the values of two operands are equal.	(C == D) is not true.
!=	Checks whether the values of two operands are equal; if they aren't, Condition returns true.	(C != D) is true.
>	Checks whether the left operand's value is greater than the right operand's value; if it is, Condition is true.	(C > D) is not true.
<	Checks whether the left operand's value is smaller than the right operand's value; if it is, Condition is true.	(C < D) is true.
>=	If the left operand's value is larger than or equal to the right operand's value, then Condition is true.	(C >= D) is not true.
<=	The Condition is true if the left operand's value is less than or equal to the right operand's value.	(C <= D) is true.

Logical Operators

Operator	Description	Example
&&	The logical AND operator is what it's called. The condition becomes true when both operands are non-zero.	(C && D) is false.
||	The logical OR operator is what it's called. Condition is true if one of the two operands is non-zero.	(C || D) is true.
!	It's known as the Logical NOT Operator. Its operand's logical state is reversed when it is used. The Logical NOT operator returns false if a condition is true.	!(C && D) is true.

Bitwise Operators

p	q	p & q	p | q	p ^ q
0	0	0	0	0
0	1	0	1	1
1	1	1	1	0
1	0	0	1	1

Assignment Operators

Operator	Description	Example
=	The assignment operator is simple. Values from the right side operands are assigned to the left side operand.	A = C + D will assign value of C + D into A
+=	Using the assignment operator AND, The right operand is added to the left operand, and the result is assigned to the left operand.	A += C is equivalent to A = A + C
-=	AND (subtract AND) (assignment) (subtract AND) (a The right operand is subtracted from the left operand, and the result is assigned to the left operand.	A -= C is equivalent to A = A - C
*=	The multiply AND assignment operator adds the right and left operands together and assigns the result to the left operand.	C *= A is equivalent to C = C * A
/=	Divide AND assignment operator: It divides the left operand with the right operand and assigns the result to the left operand.	A /= C is equivalent to A = A / C
%=	The assignment operator AND the modulus, uses two operands to calculate the modulus and assigns the result to the left operand.	A %= C is equivalent to A = A % C
<<=	Left shift AND assignment operator.	A <<= 2 is same as A = A << 2
>>=	Right shift AND assignment operator.	A >>= 2 is same as A = A >> 2
&=	Bitwise AND assignment operator.	A &= 2 is same as A = A & 2
^=	Bitwise exclusive OR and assignment operator.	A ^= 2 is same as A = A ^ 2
|=	Bitwise inclusive OR and assignment operator.	A |= 2 is same as A = A | 2

Misc Operators

Sr. No	Operator and Description
1	**sizeof** The sizeof operation returns the variable's size. For instance, sizeof(a), where an is an integer, returns 4.
2	**Condition? X : Y** (?) is a conditional operator. If Condition is true, the value of X is returned; otherwise, the value of Y is returned.
3	, A sequence of operations is done when the comma operator is used. The value of the whole comma expression is the value of the comma-separated list's last expression.
4	**. (dot) and -> (arrow)** Individual members of classes, structures, and unions are referenced using member operators.
5	**Cast** Casting operations change the data type of a variable. Int(2.2000) would, for example, yield 2.
6	**&** The address of a variable is returned by the pointer operator. For example, &a; will return the variable's real address.
7	* A variable is pointed to by the pointer operator *. For example, *var; refers to the variable var.

OPERATORS PRECEDENCE

The request in which terms in an expression are gathered is dictated by operator precedence. This affects how a word is judged. Certain administrators take need over others; the duplication administrator, for instance, outweighs the expansion administrator.

Category	Operator	Associativity
Postfix	() [] ->. ++ - -	Left to right
Unary	+ - ! ˜ ++ - - (type)* & sizeof	Right to left
Multiplicative	* / %	Left to right
Additive	+ –	Left to right
Shift	<< >>	Left to right
Relational	< <= > >=	Left to right
Equality	== !=	Left to right
Bitwise AND	&	Left to right
Bitwise XOR	^	Left to right
Bitwise OR	|	Left to right
Logical AND	&&	Left to right
Logical OR	||	Left to right
Conditional	?:	Right to left
Assignment	= += -= *= /= %=>>= <<= &= ^= |=	Right to left
Comma	,	Left to right

LOOP IN C++

You could find yourself in a situation where you need to run a code block many times. Statements are usually executed in the following order: the first statement in a function is executed first, followed by the second, and so on.

Programming languages offer a variety of control structures, allowing for more complicated execution paths.

Sr. No	Loop Type & Description
1	while loop While a given condition is true, it repeats a statement or a set of assertions. Before performing the loop body, it checks the condition.
2	for loop The code that controls the loop variable is abbreviated by executing a sequence of instructions numerous times.
3	do...while loop It's similar to a 'while' statement, except it checks the condition at the conclusion of the loop body.
4	nested loops One or more loops can be used within another 'while,' 'for,' or 'do.. while.' loop.

Control Statements for Loops

Control statements in loops alter the execution sequence. All automated objects generated in scope are deleted when execution exits that scope.

Sr. No	Control Statement and Description
1	break statement
	The loop or switch statement is terminated, and execution is transferred to the statement immediately after the loop or switch.
2	continue statement
	It forces the loop to skip the rest of its body and retest its state immediately before repeating.
3	goto statement
	Control is passed to the labeled statement. However, using a goto statement in your program is not recommended.

Infinite Loop

A loop becomes infinite if a condition never becomes false. The for loop is commonly used for this. Because none of the three expressions that make up the 'for' loop are required, you may create an endless loop by leaving the conditional expression empty.

Example:

```
#include <iostream>
using namespace std;

int main () {
    for( ; ; ) {
        printf("Loop will forever run. \n");
    }

    return 0;
}
```

DECISION-MAKING STATEMENTS

The software engineer should portray at most minuscule one Condition that the program will assess or test, just as an articulation or explanations that will be executed if the condition is valid. Alternatively, further proclamations will be achieved if the condition is false.

Sr. No	Statement & Description
1	if statement A Boolean expression is followed by one or more statements in an if statement.
2	if...else statement When the Boolean expression is false, a 'if' statement might be followed by an optional 'else' statement.
3	switch statement A switch statement allows a variable to be compared against a list of values for equality.
4	nested if statements One if or else if statement can be used inside another if or else if statement.
5	nested switch statements One 'switch' statement can be used inside another 'switch' statement.

CONDITIONAL OPERATOR?

Syntax:

```
Exp1? Exp2 : Exp3;
```

Expressions Exp1, Exp2, and Exp3 are used. Take note of the colon's use and location. The value of a? expression is calculated in the following way: Exp1 is evaluated. If this is the case, Exp2 is evaluated, and the value of the entire? Expression is determined. If Exp1 is false, Exp3 is considered, and its value is used as the expression's value.

Example:

```cpp
#include <iostream>
using namespace std;

int main () {
    // Local variable declaration:
    int a, b = 20;

    a = (b < 20)?  30 : 50;
    cout << "The value of a: " << a << endl;

    return 0;
}
```

Output:

```
The value of a: 50
```

FUNCTIONS IN C++

A function is a group of statements that cooperate to perform a task. Every C++ program has at least one function, main (), and even the simplest program can have many functions specified.

You may break your code into different functions. It's up to you how you split your code into separate functions, but logically; each function should be doing a specific purpose.

The name, return type, and parameters of a function are all specified in a function declaration. A function definition defines the body of the function.

Function Defining

```
return_type function_name( parameter
list ) {
   body of the function
}
```

A function definition in C++ is made up of two parts: a function header and a function body.

- **Return Type:** As its return type, a function can return a value. The data type of the value returned by the function is specified by the return type. Some functions perform as expected but do not return a value. In this case, the return type is referred to as void.

- **Function Name:** This is the function's actual name. The function signature is made up of the function name and the argument list.

- **Parameters:** A placeholder is what a parameter is. When you call a capacity, you send a value to the contention. This value is referred to by the actual parameter or argument. The boundary list refers to the kind, request, and a number of capacity boundaries. Parameters are optional; they might be present in a capacity.

- **Function Body:** The function body is made up of a series of explanations that show how the capability works.

Example:

```
int maxi(int number1, int number2) {
   // local variable declaration
   int result;
```

```
    if (number1 > number2)
        result = number1;
    else
        result = number2;

    return result;
}
```

Declarations of Functions

A function declaration gives the compiler the name of the function and how to invoke it.

Syntax:

```
return_type function_name( parameter
list );
```

Making a Function Call

When you create a C++ function, you must define what the function must perform. You must call or invoke a function before you may utilize it.

When a program calls a function, control is passed from the calling program to the called function. A function performs a defined job and then returns program control to the main program when its return statement is executed or its function-ending closing brace is reached.

Arguments for Functions

On the off chance that a capacity will use arguments, it needs to characterize factors that will take the values of the arguments. These factors are known as the function's formal parameters.

The formal parameters are produced when the capacity is entered and erased when left, very much like any nearby factors inside the function.

Sr. No	Call Type and Description
1	Call by Value
	This technique replicates an argument's real value into the function's formal parameter. Changes to the parameter inside the function have no effect on the argument in this situation.
2	Call by Pointer
	The address of an argument is copied into the formal parameter using this approach. The address is utilized within the function to retrieve the actual parameter used in the call. This implies that changes to the parameter have an impact on the argument.
3	Call by Reference
	This method copies the reference of an argument into the formal parameter. Inside the function, the reference is used to access the actual argument used in the call. This means that changes made to the parameter affect the argument.

Parameters Default Values

You might give a default worth to every one of the last contentions when you characterize a capacity. If the comparing parameters are left clear while conjuring the capacity, this worth will be used.

This is accomplished by assigning value to the parameters in the capacity definition utilizing the task administrator. When the capacity is called without an incentive for that contention, the default offered some benefit is used; in any case, if a worth is determined, the default esteem is overlooked, and the passed estimation has utilized all things considered.

Example:

```cpp
#include <iostream>
using namespace std;

int sum(int x, int y = 10) {
    int result;
    result = x + y;

    return (result);
}
int main () {
    // local variable declaration:
    int x = 50;
    int y = 100;
    int result;

    // calling a function to add the
values.
    result = sum(x, y);
    cout << "Total value :" << Result <<
endl;

    // calling a function again as follows.
    result = sum(a);
    cout << "Total value :" << Result <<
endl;

    return 0;
}
```

Output:

```
Total value: 150
Total value: 60
```

NUMBERS IN C++

We utilize crude information types like int, short, long, buoy, and twofold when working with Numbers. While talking about C++ Data Types, the number information types, their possible qualities, and number reaches were clarified.

Numbers Defining

- i = 1000;

- l = 1000000;

- f = 230.47;

Math Operations

C++ contains a large number of mathematical operations that may be applied to a variety of integers.

Sr. No	Function and Purpose
1	**double cos(double);** This method returns the cosine of an angle (as a double).
2	**double sin(double);** This method returns the sine from an angle (as a double).
3	**double tan(double);** This function takes an angle (as a double) and returns the tangent.
4	**double log(double);** This function accepts an integer and returns the number's natural logarithm.
5	**double pow(double, double);** The first is a number you'd want to increase, and the second is the amount of power you'd like to gain.
6	**double hypot(double, double);** The hypotenuse length will be returned if you provide this function the length of two sides of a right triangle.

(Continued)

Sr. No	Function and Purpose
7	**double sqrt(double);** This function takes an integer and returns the square root.
8	**int abs(int);** The absolute value of an integer supplied to this method is returned.
9	**double fabs(double);** The absolute value of any decimal number provided to this method is returned.
10	**double floor(double);** Finds the smallest or largest integer that is less than or equal to the input.

Example:

```cpp
#include <iostream>
#include <cmath>
using namespace std;

int main () {
    // number definition:
    short  s = 10;
    long   l = 100000;
    float  f = 20.47;

    // mathematical operations;
    cout << "sin(d) :" << sin(d) << endl;
    cout << "abs(i)  :" << abs(i) << endl;
    return 0;
}
```

ARRAYS

In C++, an array is a data structure that stores a fixed-size sequential collection of objects of the same type in fixed-size sequential order. Although an array is used to store data, it is often more convenient to think of it as a collection of similar-type variables.

Rather than defining individual variables like number0, number1,..., and number49, you declare a single array variable called numbers and use numbers[0], numbers[1],..., numbers[49] to represent individual variables.

Syntax:

```
type arrayName [ arraySize ];
```

Sr. No	Description
1	Multidimensional arrays
	Multidimensional arrays are supported in C++. The two-dimensional array is the most basic type of multidimensional array.
2	Pointer to an array
	Simply giving the array name without any index will create a reference to the first member of the array.
3	Passing arrays to functions
	By supplying the array's name without an index, you can send a reference to the method.
4	Return array from functions
	A function in C++ can return an array.

STRINGS

There are two different sorts of string representations.

1. The character string is in C style.

2. Standard C++ introduces the string class type.

Character String

The character string was concocted in the C programming language is as yet upheld in C++. This string is a one-dimensional cluster of characters, with the invalid person '0' toward the end. An invalid-ended string, then again, incorporates the characters that make up the string, trailed by null.

```
char a[5] = {'H', 'e', 'l', 'l', 'o'};
```

Example:

```cpp
#include <iostream>
using namespace std;
int main () {
    char a[5] = {'H', 'e', 'l', 'l', 'o',};
    cout << "Message: ";
    cout << a << endl;
    return 0;
}
```

Output:

```
Message: Hello
```

Null-terminated string manipulation functions include:

Sr. No	Function
1	**strcpy(s1, s2);** String s2 is copied into string s1.
2	**strcat(s1, s2);** String s2 is appended to the end of string s1.
3	**strlen(s1);** The length of string s1 is returned.
4	**strcmp(s1, s2);** If s1 and s2 are equal, returns 0; less than 0 if s1s2; larger than 0 if s1>s2.

(Continued)

Sr. No	Function
5	**strchr(s1, ch);** The first occurrence of the character ch in string s1 is returned as a pointer.
6	**strstr(s1, s2);** A pointer is returned for the first occurrence of string s2 in string s1.

String Class

The library includes a string class type that supports all of the operations listed above and a lot more.

Example:

```cpp
#include <iostream>
#include <string>

using namespace std;

int main () {

    string str1 = "Hello";
    string str2;
    int  len;

    // copy str1 into str2
    Str2 = str1;
    cout << "str2 : " << str2 << endl;
    return 0;
}
```

Output:

```
Str2: Hello
```

POINTERS

C++ pointers are easy to understand and use, and while some C++ tasks are simpler with them, others, such as dynamic memory allocation, cannot be done without them.

A pointer is a variable whose value is the location of another variable. Before using a pointer, just like any other variable or consistent, it should be pronounced.

Syntax:

```
type *var-name;
```

The asterisk bullet you used to proclaim a pointer is likewise the asterisk you use to duplicate.

```
float   *fp;    // pointer to a float
char    *ch     // pointer to character
```

Sr. No	Description
1	Null Pointers
	Null pointer, a constant with a zero value defined in various standard libraries, is supported in C++.
2	Pointer Arithmetic
	On pointers, the arithmetic operators ++, --, +, and - can be utilized.
3	Pointers vs. Arrays
	Pointers and arrays have a very close relationship.
4	Array of Pointers
	Arrays can be used to hold many pointers.
5	Pointer to Pointer
	You can have a pointer on a pointer in C++, and so on.

(Continued)

Sr. No	Description
6	Passing Pointers to Functions
	Passing an argument by reference or by address allows the called function to modify the supplied argument in the calling code.
7	Return Pointer from Functions
	A function in C++ can return a pointer to a local variable, a static variable, or dynamically allocated memory.

DATE AND TIME

The C++ standard library lacks a suitable data type, therefore it inherits the structs and methods for handling dates and times from C. To access date and time-related functions and structures in your C++ application, you must include the ctime> header file.

The four time-related types are clock t, time t, size t, and tm. To express the system time and date as an integer, use the clock t, size t, and time t types.

Example:

```
struct tm {
    int tm_mon;
    int tm_year;
    int tm_wday;
    int tm_yday;
}
```

Sr. No	Function
1	**time_t time(time_t *time);**
	This returns the system's current calendar time as a number of seconds since January 1, 1970. If the system does not have any time, a value of.1 is returned.
2	**char *ctime(const time_t *time);**
	This function produces a string of the form day month year hours:minutes:seconds year\n\0.

(Continued)

Sr. No	Function
3	**struct tm *localtime(const time_t *time);** This gives you a pointer to the tm structure, which is used to indicate local time.
4	**clock_t clock(void);** This gives you a rough estimate of how long the calling application has been running. If the time is unavailable, a value of.1 is returned.
5	**char * asctime (const struct tm * time);** This returns a reference to a string containing the data contained in the structure pointed to by time, which has been transformed to the form: date (day, month) seconds: minutes: hours: minutes: hours: minutes: minutes: minutes: minutes: minutes year\n\0.
6	**struct tm *gmtime(const time_t *time);** This returns a tm structure with a reference to the time. Coordinated Universal Time (UTC), which is basically Greenwich Mean Time, is used to indicate the time (GMT).
7	**time_t mktime(struct tm *time);** The calendar-time equivalent of the time in the structure referenced to by time is returned.
8	**double difftime (time_t time2, time_t time1);** The difference in seconds between time1 and time2 is calculated using this function.
9	**size_t strftime();** This function allows you to format the date and time in a specified way.

BASIC INPUT/OUTPUT

Input/Output occurs in streams, which are byte-by-byte successions. The progression of bytes from a gadget like a console, a circle drive, or an organization association with principle memory is known as info, while the progression of bytes from fundamental memory to a gadget, for example, a presentation screen, a printer, a plate drive, or an organization association is known as yield.

Sr. No	Header File and Function
1	**<iostream>**
	The cin, cout, cerr, and clog objects are defined in this file, and they correspond to the standard input stream, standard output stream, un-buffered standard error stream, and buffered standard error stream, respectively.
2	**<iomanip>**
	This file declares services like setw and set precision that are helpful for conducting formatted I/O using so-called parameterized stream manipulators.
3	**<fstream>**
	This file defines user-controlled file processing services.

DATA STRUCTURES

Data structures are a huge and unavoidable element of any programming project. Cells, the tiniest unit of life, are just as reliant on us humans for a variety of biological processes. The basic unit of programming known as "data" underpins the whole C++ program. The implementation of data structures allows us to conduct data operations such as data representation, storage, organization, and many others in a meaningful way.

An information type is just an assortment of comparable information with a similar name. Comparable information types have comparable properties and act comparatively, like taking up a similar measure of PC memory and serving a similar capacity.

There are two significant kinds of information:

1. **Primitive data type:** These information types are otherwise called crude information types. These are pre-characterized information types that give the

C++ compiler a particular significance. For example, int, coast, singe, string, double, etc.

2. **Non-primitive data type:** These information types are comprised of crude information types. Since they are not pre-characterized by the C++ compiler, they are at times known as client characterized information types. Arrays, structures, unions, classes, linked lists, enumeration, etc., are models.

Data Structures of Various Types

The usage of C++ data structures allows a programmer to mix different data types in a group and process them as a single unit, making things more easy and understandable.

In C++, data structures are divided into three categories.

1. **Simple:** In C++, these data structures are usually made up of primitive data types like int, float, double, string, and char.

2. **Compound:** These sorts of data structures can be created by merging simple data structures. It is further divided into two categories:

   • **Linear data structure:** A data structure is considered to be linear if its elements are arranged in a logical order.

   • **Non-linear data structure:** Multilevel data structures are non-linear data structures.

3. **Static and Dynamic:** Static data structures have a constant size and structure connected with some specified memory locations that are fixed at compilation time. For instance, consider arrays.

Data Structures Operations

- **Insertion:** Inserting a new data element into the data structure is referred to as this operation.

- **Deletion:** In the data structure, delete or remove an existing data element.

- **Traversal:** Process and display all data pieces in the data structure using traversal.

- **Searching:** Look through the data structure for a certain data element.

- **Sorting:** Sort the data items in the data structure in ascending or descending order, or in any other logically sequential order.

- **Merging:** It is the process of combining similar data pieces from two or more data structures to create a new data structure.

OBJECT ORIENTED

Classes and Objects in C++

The fundamental goal of C++ programming is to introduce object orientation to the C programming language, and classes, also known as user-defined types, are the key element of C++ that allows object-oriented programming.

A class specifies an object's form by combining data representation and methods for changing that data into a single package. Members of a class are the data and methods that make up the class.

Class Definitions in C++

When you define a class, you're essentially defining a data type's blueprint. This doesn't specify any data, but it does define what the class name implies, that is, what a class object will be made up of and what actions can be done on it.

The keyword class is used to start a class definition, followed by the class name, and lastly the class body, which is enclosed by a pair of curly brackets. A semicolon or a series of declarations must come after a class definition. For example, we used the term class to define the Box data type:

Example:

```
class B {
    public:
        double length;
        double breadth;
        double height;
};
```

The access characteristics of the members of the class that follows it are determined by the keyword public. Anywhere inside the scope of the class object, a public member can be accessed from outside the class. You may also make a class's members secret or protected, which we'll cover in a later section.

C++ Objects

A class serves as the blueprint for things, thus an object is essentially produced from one. Objects of a class are declared in the same way as variables of fundamental types are declared. The following statements declare two Car objects:

```
Car Car1;
Car Car2;
```

Members Having Access to Data

The direct member access operator may be used to access the public data members of a class's objects (.). To clarify matters, consider the following example:

```cpp
#include <iostream>
using namespace std;

class box {
    public:
        double length;
        double breadth;
        double height;
};

int main() {
    box box1;
    box box2;
    double volume = 0.3;

    // specification
    box1.height = 3.0;
    box1.length = 4.0;
    box1.breadth = 7.0;

    // specification
    box2.height = 20.0;
    box2.length = 21.0;
    box2.breadth = 14.0;

    // volume
    volume = box1.height * box1.length *
    box1.breadth;
    cout << "The Volume of box1: " << volume
    <<endl;
```

```
// volume of box 2
volume = box2.height * box2.length *
box2.breadth;
cout << "The Volume of box2: " << volume
<<endl;
return 0;
}
```

Output:

```
The Volume of box1: 84
The Volume of box2: 5880
```

It's crucial to know that the direct member access operator cannot access private or protected members (.). We'll discover how to gain access to secret and protected users.

Detail on Classes and Objects

So far, you've learned the fundamentals of C++ Classes and Objects. There are a few more fascinating ideas linked to C++ Classes and Objects that we'll go over in the following sub-sections:

Sr. No	Description
1	Functions of Class Members: A member function of a class is a function that, like any other variable, has its definition or prototype within the class declaration.
2	Modifiers for Class Access: A class member can be made public, private, or protected. Members are presumed to be private by default.
3	Constructor and Destructor: A class function is a specific function in a class that is called when a new object of that class is created. A destructor is a specific function that is run when an object is created and then destroyed.

(Continued)

Sr. No	Description
4	Copy Constructor: The copy function is a function that produces an object by initialising it using a previously generated object of the same class.
5	Friend Functions: A friend function has full access to a class's private and protected members.
6	Inline Functions: In the case of an inline function, the compiler tries to extend the code in the body of the function rather than calling it.
7	this Pointer: Every object has a unique pointer that refers to the actual object.
8	Pointer: A class pointer is created in the same manner as a structure pointer is created. In reality, a class is nothing more than a structure containing functions.
9	Static Members: A class's data and function members can both be declared static.

Inheritance

The idea of inheritance is one of the most essential in object-oriented programming. Inheritance enables us to define a class in terms of another class, which simplifies application development and maintenance. This also allows for the reuse of code functionality and a quick implementation time.

Instead of developing entirely new data members and member methods when establishing a class, the programmer can specify that the new class should inherit the members of an existing class. The current class is known as the base class, while the new class is known as the derived class. Inheritance is a connection that is implemented.

Base and Derived Classes

A class can be derived from several base classes, allowing it to inherit data and functionalities from various sources.

To provide the base class for a derived class, we utilize a class derivation list. A class derivation list takes the form and names one or more base classes.

```
class derivedclass: access-specifier baseclass
```

Where base-class is the name of a previously created class and access-specifier is one of public, protected, or private. It is private by default if the access-specifier is not used.

Example:

```cpp
#include <iostream>

using namespace std;

// Class-Base
class shape {
   public:
      void setWidth(int w) {
         wd = w;
      }
      void setHeight(int h) {
         hg = h;
      }

   protected:
      int wd;
      int hg;
};

// Derived-class
class rect: public shape {
   public:
```

```cpp
        int getArea() {
            return (wd * hg);
        }
};

int main(void) {
    rect r;

    r.setWidth(5);
    r.setHeight(7);

    // Print
    cout << "The Total area: " <<
r.getArea() << endl;

    return 0;
}
```

Output:

```
The Total area: 35
```

Inheritance and Access Control

A derived class has access to all of its base class's non-private members. As a result, any base-class elements that should not be available to derived class member functions should be made private in the base class.

The different access kinds can be summarized in the following fashion based on who has access to them:

Access	public	protected	private
Same class	yes	yes	yes
Derived classes	yes	yes	no
Outside classes	yes	no	no

With the exclusions listed below, a derived class inherits all base class methods.

- The base class's constructors, destructors, and copy constructors.

- The base class's operators are overloaded.

- The base class's friend functions.

Types

When creating a class from a base class, the base class can be inherited in one of three ways: public, protected, or private inheritance. As previously stated, the access-specifier specifies the type of inheritance.

Protected and private inheritance is rarely utilized, while public inheritance is. The following principles apply when utilizing various types of inheritance:

- **Public class:** When a class is derived from a public base class, the base class's public members become public members of the derived class, and the base class's protected members become protected members of the derived class. The private members of a base class are never directly available from a derived class, although they can be accessed via calls to the base class's public and protected members.

- **Protected Inheritance:** When a derived class inherits from a protected base class, the base class's public and protected members become protected members of the derived class.

- **Private Inheritance:** When a derived class is derived from a private base class, the base class's public and protected members become private members of the derived class.

Multiple Inheritance

A C++ class can inherit members from multiple classes, and the expanded syntax is as follows:

```
class derivedclass: access baseC, access
baseD.
```

Where access is one of **public, protected,** or **private** and would be given for every base class and they will be separated by comma as shown above. Let us try the following example

Example:

```
#include <iostream>

using namespace std;

// Base class
class shape
{
   public:
       void setWidth(int w) {
          wd = w;
       }
       void setHeight(int h)
{
          hg = h;
       }
```

```cpp
    protected:
        int wd;
        int hg;
};

// Base class
class paintcost {
    public:
        int getCost(int ar) {
            return ar * 30;
        }
};

// Derived class
class Rect: public shape, public
paintcost {
    public:
        int getArea() {
            return (wd * hg);
        }
};

int main(void) {
    Rect r;
    int ar;

  r.setWidth(7);
    r.setHeight(8);

    ar = r.getArea();

    // Print the area
    cout << "The Total area: " <<
r.getArea() << endl;
```

```
    // Print the total cost
    cout << "The Total paint cost:" <<
r.getCost(ar) << endl;

    return 0;
}
```

Output:

```
The Total area: 56
The Total paint cost:1680
```

OVERLOADING

Function overloading and operator overloading are terms used in C++ to describe the ability to specify several definitions for a function name or an operator in the same scope.

An overloaded declaration is one that has the same name as a previously declared declaration in the same scope, but both declarations have distinct parameters and clearly different definitions.

The compiler determines which definition to apply when you call an overloaded function or operator by comparing the argument types you used to invoke the function or operator to the parameter types supplied in the definitions.

Overloading Function

In C++, function overloading means that the same function name can have several definitions in the same scope. The kinds and/or the number of arguments in the argument list must be different in each function declaration. Overloading function declarations that differ only in return type is not possible.

Example:

```cpp
#include <iostream>
using namespace std;

class printd {
   public:
      void print(int j) {
        cout << "Printing int: " << j
<< endl;
      }
      void print(double  h) {
        cout << "Printing float: " << h
        << endl;
      }
      void print(char* b) {
        cout << "Printing character: "
        << b << endl;
      }
};

int main(void) {
   printd pd;

   // Call print
   pd.print(4);

   // Call print
   pd.print(400.223);

   // Call print
   pd.print("Hello ");

   return 0;
}
```

Output:

```
Printing int: 4
Printing float: 400.223
Printing character: Hello
```

Overloading Operators

In C++, you may redefine or overload most of the built-in operators. As a result, a programmer may also utilize operators with user-defined types.

Overloaded operators are functions with unique names, consisting of the keyword "operator" followed by the symbol for the operator to be defined. An overloaded operator, like any other function, has a return type and an argument list.

Syntax:

```
box operator+(const box&);
```

defines the addition operator, which may be used to combine two Box instances and yields the resultant Box object The majority of overloaded operators may be classified as non-member functions or class member functions. If we create the above function as a non-member function of a class, we must provide two arguments for each operand, as shown below:

Syntax:

```
box operator+(const box&, const box&);
```

The following example uses a member function to demonstrate the idea of operator overloading. The object that will call this operator can be accessed using this operator as explained below: An object is passed as an argument whose properties will be accessed using this object, and the object that will call this operator can be accessed using this operator as explained below:

Example:

```
#include <iostream>
using namespace std;

class box {
   public:
      double getVolume(void) {
         return leng * bread * heig;
      }
      void setLength( double len ) {
         leng = len;
      }
      void setBreadth( double bre ) {
         bread = bre;
      }
      void setHeight( double hei ) {
         heig = hei;
      }

      // Overload + operator to add two
      Box objects.
      box operator+(const box& b) {
         box boxx;
         boxx.leng = this->leng + b.leng;
         boxx.bread = this->bread +
         b.bread;
         boxx.heig = this->heig + b.heig;
```

```cpp
        return boxx;
    }

    private:
        double leng;
        double bread;
        double heig;
};

// Main function
int main() {
    box box1;
    box box2;
    box box3;
    double volume = 0.0;

    // specification
    box1.setLength(8.0);
    box1.setBreadth(4.0);
    box1.setHeight(6.0);

    // specification
    box2.setLength(11.0);
    box2.setBreadth(14.0);
    box2.setHeight(12.0);

    // volume
    volume = box1.getVolume();
    cout << "Volume of box1 : " <<
volume <<endl;

    // volume
    volume = box2.getVolume();
    cout << "Volume of box2 : " <<
volume <<endl;
```

```
// Add two object as follows:
box3 = box1 + box2;

// volume
volume = box3.getVolume();
cout << "Volume of box3 : " <<
volume <<endl;

return 0;
}
```

Output:

```
Volume of box1: 192
Volume of box2: 1848
Volume of box3: 6156
```

Polymorphism

Polymorphism refers to the fact that something exists in several forms. Polymorphism usually happens when there is a hierarchy of classes that are connected through inheritance.

Polymorphism in C++ refers to the fact that depending on the kind of object that calls a member function, a different function is performed.

Consider the following scenario, in which a base class is derived from two additional classes:

Example:

```
#include <iostream>
using namespace std;
```

```
class shape {
   protected:
      int wd, hg;

   public:
      Shape( int w = 0, int h = 0){
         width = w;
         height = h;
      }
      int ar() {
         cout << "The Parent class area
         :" <<endl;
         return 0;
      }
};
class rectangle: public shape {
   public:
      rectangle( int w = 0, int h =
      0):Shape(w, h) { }

      int ar () {
         cout << "The Rectangle class
         area :" <<endl;
         return (wd * hg);
      }
};

class triangle: public shape {
   public:
      triangle( int w = 0, int h =
0):shape(w, h) { }

      int ar () {
         cout << "The Triangle class
         area :" <<endl;
```

```
            return (wd * hg / 2);
        }
};

// Main function
int main() {
    shape *sh;
    rectangle rc(10,7);
    triangle  tr(10,5);

    // store the address of Rectangle
    sh = &rc;

    // call rectangle area.
    sh->ar();

    // store the address of Triangle
    sh = &tr;

    // call triangle area.
    sh->ar();

    return 0;
}
```

Output:

```
The Parent class area :
The Parent class area :
```

Data Abstraction

Data abstraction refers to simply exposing important information to the outer world while hiding background details,
i.e. to represent the needed information in a programme
without displaying the intricacies.

Data abstraction is a programming approach in which the interface and implementation are separated.

Take, for example, a television, which you can turn on and off, change the channel, adjust the volume, and add external components such as speakers, DVD players, but you have no idea how it receives signals over the air or through a cable, how it translates them, and finally displays them on the screen.

As a result, we can argue that a television clearly isolates its internal implementation from its exterior interface, allowing you to interact with its interfaces such as the power button, channel changer, and volume control without knowing anything about its internals.

Classes in C++ enable a high level of data abstraction. They expose enough public methods to the outside world to allow them to experiment with the object's functionality and change object data, i.e. state, without having to know how the class is built inside.

Your application, for example, can call the sort() method without knowing what algorithm the function uses to sort the input data. In reality, the actual implementation of the sorting feature may change between library releases, but your function call will still work as long as the interface remains the same.

Example:

```
#include <iostream>
using namespace std;

int main() {
    cout << "Hello " <<endl;
    return 0;
}
```

You don't need to know how cout displays text on the user's screen in this case. You just need to understand the public interface; the underlying implementation of 'cout' can be changed at any time.

Data Abstraction's Advantages
Data abstraction has two major advantages.

1. Inadvertent user-level mistakes that might damage the object's state are shielded from class internals.

2. Without requiring changes to user-level code, the class implementation may develop over time in response to new needs or problem reports.

The class author is able to alter the data by defining data members only in the private part of the class. If the implementation changes, all that has to be done is look at the class code to determine what impact the change could have. Any function that directly accesses the data members of the previous representation may be broken if the data is public.

Data abstraction may be seen in any C++ program that implements a class with public and private members.

Example:

```cpp
#include <iostream>
using namespace std;

class Add {
    public:
```

```cpp
        // constructor
        Add(int a = 0) {
            t = a;
        }

        // interface to outside world
        void addNumb(int num) {
            t += num;
        }

        int getTotal() {
            return t;
        };

    private:
        // hidden data
        int t;
};

int main() {
    Add ad;

    ad.addNumb(10);
    ad.addNumb(20);
    ad.addNumb(30);

    cout << "Total: " << ad.getTotal()
    <<endl;
    return 0;
}
```

Output:

```
Total: 60
```

Encapsulation

The following two essential components are present in all C++ programs:

Functions are the parts of a program that perform actions, and they are termed program statements.

Program data is the program's information that is influenced by the program's functions.

Encapsulation is a notion in Object Oriented Programming that ties together data and the functions that change it, keeping both protected from outside intervention and misuse. The essential OOP idea of data hiding was born from data encapsulation.

Data abstraction is a technique for exposing only the interfaces and hiding the implementation details from the user, whereas data encapsulation is a strategy for packaging data and the functions that utilize it.

Encapsulation and data hiding are supported in C++ via the use of classes, which are user-defined types. We've previously seen that a class can have members who are secret, protected, or public. All items declared in a class are private by default.

Example:

```
class box {
   public:
      double getVol(void) {
         return len * bread * heig;
      }

   private:
      double len;
```

```
        double bread;
        double heig;
    };
```

The length, width, and height variables are all private. This implies that they can only be accessible by other Box class members and not by any other component of your application. This is one method of encapsulation.

You must define sections of a class after the public keyword to make them public (i.e., available to other parts of your program). All other functions in your application can access any variables or functions declared after the public specifier.

By making one class a buddy of another, the implementation details are exposed and encapsulation is lost. The ideal situation is to keep as many of each class's information hidden from other classes as possible.

Example:

```
#include <iostream>
using namespace std;

class Add {
    public:
        // constructor
        Add(int a = 0) {
            total = a;
        }

        // interface
        void addNum(int numb) {
            total += numb;
        }
```

```cpp
        // interface
        int getTotal() {
           return total;
        };

   private:
      // hidden data
      int total;
};

int main() {
   Add ad;

   ad.addNum(20);
   ad.addNum(30);
   ad.addNum(10);

   cout << "Total: " << ad.getTotal()
   <<endl;
   return 0;
}
```

Output:

```
Total: 60
```

The total of the numbers in the above class is returned. The public members addNum and getTotal are the class's external interfaces, and a user must be familiar with them in order to utilize it. The private member total is hidden from the rest of the world, yet it is required for the class to function properly.

Interfaces

An interface specifies a C++ class's behavior or capabilities without committing to a specific implementation of that class.

Abstract classes are used to implement C++ interfaces. These abstract classes should not be confused with data abstraction, which is a notion that separates implementation details from related data.

A class becomes abstract when at least one of its functions is declared as a pure virtual function. The expression "= 0" in the declaration of a pure virtual function is as follows:

Example:

```
class box {
    public:
        // virtual function
        virtual double getVol() = 0;

    private:
        double len;        // Box Length
        double bread;      // Box Breadth
        double heig;       // Box Height
};
```

An abstract class (also known as an ABC) is used to provide a suitable foundation class from which further classes can be derived. Abstract classes are solely used as a user interface and cannot be utilized to create objects. A compilation error occurs when an object of an abstract class is attempted to be instantiated.

As a result, if an ABC subclass has to be created, it must implement each of the virtual functions, implying that it supports the ABC's interface. Compilation errors occur when a derived class fails to override a pure virtual function before attempting to create instances of that class.

Example:

```cpp
#include <iostream>
using namespace std;

// Base class
class shape {
   public:
       // pure virtual function
       virtual int getAr() = 0;
       void setWidth(int wd) {
          wid = wd;
       }

       void setHeight(int hg) {
          hei = hg;
       }

   protected:
       int wid;
       int hei;
};

// Derived class
class rectangle: public shape {
   public:
       int getAr() {
           return (wid * hei);
```

```cpp
        }
};

class triangle: public shape {
    public:
        int getAr() {
            return (wid * hei)/2;
        }
};

int main(void) {
    rectangle rect;
    triangle  tri;

    rect.setWidth(6);
    rect.setHeight(4);

    // Print
    cout << "The Total Rectangle area: "
    << rect.getAr() << endl;

    tri.setWidth(5);
    tri.setHeight(7);

    // Print
    cout << "The Total Triangle area: "
    << tri.getAr() << endl;

    return 0;
}
```

Output:

```
The Total Rectangle area: 24
The Total Triangle area: 17
```

HOW TO WORK WITH FILE TAKING CARE OF IN C++?

Following pointers will be canvassed:

- Opening a File

- Keeping in touch with a File

- Perusing from a File

- Close a File

Document Handling in C++

Documents are utilized to store information in a capacity gadget for all time. Document taking care of gives a component to store the yield of a program in a record and to perform the different procedures on it.

A stream is a deliberation that addresses a gadget on which activities of information and yield are performed. A stream can be addressed as a source or objective of characters of endless length relying upon its use.

In C++ we have a bunch of record-taking care techniques. These incorporate ifstream, ofstream, and fstream. These classes are gotten from fstrembase and the relating iostream class. These classes, intended to deal with the circle documents, are proclaimed in fstream, and hence we should incorporate fstream, and subsequently, we should remember this record for any program that utilizations records.

In C++, documents are primarily managed by utilizing three classes fstream, ifstream, ofstream.

- **ofstream:** This Stream class means the yield document stream and is applied to make records for composing data to records

- **ifstream:** This Stream class connotes the information document stream and is applied for perusing data from records

- **fstream:** This Stream class can be utilized for both peruse and compose from/to documents.

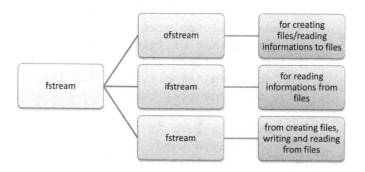

In C++, documents are primarily managed by utilizing three classes

Source Code:

```
/* File Handling with C++ using
ifstream & ofstream */
/* To write the Content */
/* Read the content*/

#include <iostream>
#include <fstream>
```

```cpp
using namespace std;

// Driver Code
int main()
{

    // Creation of ofstream class object
    ofstream fout;

    string line;

    // by default ios::out mode,
    automatically deletes
    // the content of file. To append
    the content, open in ios:app
    // fout.open("sample.txt", ios::app)
    fout.open("sample1.txt");

    // Execute a loop If file
    successfully opened
    while (fout) {

        // Read a Line from standard input
        getline(cin, line);

        // Press -1 to exit
        if (line == "-1")
                break;

        // Write line in file
        fout << This is a line << endl;
    }

    // Close the File
    fout.close();
```

```
// Creation of ifstream class object
to read the file
ifstream fin;

// by default open mode = ios::in mode
fin.open("sample1.txt");

// Execute a loop until EOF (End of
File)
while (fin) {

    // Read a Line from File
    getline(fin, line);

    // Print line in Console
    cout << line << endl;
}

// Close the file
fin.close();

return 0;
}
```

All the over three classes are gotten from fstreambase and the comparing iostream class and they are planned explicitly to oversee circle documents.

C++ gives us the accompanying tasks in File Handling:

- **Making a record:** open()

- **Understanding information:** read()

- **Composing new information:** write()

- **Shutting a document:** close()

File Handling in C++

- **Opening a File:** The principal action done on an item of one of these types is, for the most part, to connect it to a real document.

  We can open a document utilizing any of the accompanying strategies:

  1. First is bypassing the document name in the constructor at the hour of item creation.

  2. Second is utilizing the open() work.

  To open a record:

  ```
  open()
  ```

  Syntax:

  ```
  void open(const char* file_
  name,ios::openmode mode);
  ```

Modes	Description
in	The file is opened for reading.
out	Opens the file that will be written to.
binary	The file is opened in binary mode.
app	Opens the file and, at the end, appends all of the outputs.
ate	The file is opened, and the control is moved to the end of the file.
trunc	The data in the existing file is deleted.
nocreate	If the file already exists, it will be opened.
noreplace	If the file does not already exist, it is opened.

Syntax:

```
fstream new_file;
new_file.open("newfile.txt", ios::out);
```

In the above model, new_file is an object of type fstream, as we probably are aware fstream is a class, so we need to make an object of this class to utilize its part capacities. So we make the new_file article and call open() work. Here we use the mode that permits us to open the document to write in it.

Default Open Modes:

```
ifstream ios::in
ofstream ios::out
fstream ios::in | ios::out
```

Syntax:

```
ofstream new_file;
new_file.open("new_file.txt", ios::out
| ios::app );
```

Here, input mode and attach mode are consolidated, which addresses the document is opened for composing and adding the yields toward the end.

When the program ends, the memory is eradicated, opens up the memory allotted, and shuts the opened documents.

It is smarter to utilize the nearby() capacity to close the opened documents after the utilization of the record.

Utilizing a stream inclusion administrator

- **<<:** Using stream extraction administrator, we may assemble data into a document.

- **>>:** We can read data from a record with relative ease.

An example of how to use the open() method to open/create a file is as follows:

```cpp
#include<iostream>
#include <fstream>
using namespace std;
int main()
{
fstream new_file;
new_file.open("new_file",ios::out);
if(!new_file)
{
cout<<"creation failed";
}
else
{
cout<<"New file created";
new_file.close(); // Step 4: Closing
file
}
return 0;
}
```

Output:

```
New file created
```

- **Writing to a File**

  Source Code:

```cpp
#include <iostream>
#include <fstream>
using namespace std;
int main()
```

```
{
fstream new_file;
new_file.open("new_file_write.
txt",ios::out);
if(!new_file)
{
cout<<"File creation failed";
}
else
{
cout<<"New file created";
new_file<<"Learning";    //Writing to
file
new_file.close();
}
return 0;
}
```

Output:

```
New file created
```

```
*new_file_write - Notepad          —    □    ×
File  Edit  Format  View  Help
Learning
```

- **Reading from a File**

```
#include <iostream>
#include <fstream>
using namespace std;
int main()
{
fstream new_file;
```

```
new_file.open("new_file_write.
txt",ios::in);
if(!new_file)
cout<<"No such file"; } else { char ch;
while (!new_file.eof()) { new_file >>ch;
cout << ch;
}
new_file.close();
return 0;
}
```

- **Close a File:** It is just finished with the assistance of close() work.

Syntax:

```
File Pointer.close()
```

Source Code:

```
#include <iostream>
#include <fstream>
using namespace std;
int main()
{
fstream new_file;
new_file.open("new_file.
txt",ios::out);
new_file.close();
return 0;
}
```

Output:

```
The file gets closed.
```

THE MOST EFFECTIVE METHOD TO IMPLEMENT DATA ABSTRACTION IN C++

Information Abstraction is showing fundamental data to the client yet concealing the foundation subtleties.

Abstraction in C++

Think about a model: An individual uses a cell phone except if he is from an IT or ECE foundation, he knows nothing other than what catches to press. This is a legitimate illustration of Data Abstraction.

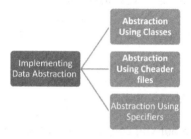

There are three different ways of executing Data Abstraction in C++:

- Abstraction Using Classes

- Abstraction utilizing header documents

- Abstraction Using Specifiers

    - **Private:** Abstraction in C++:

At the point when information part or part works are made private, it must be gotten to inside the class and nobody outside the class can get to it.

- **Public:** Abstraction in C++: When information part or part works are disclosed, it very well may be gotten to by everybody.

- **Protected:** Abstraction in C++: A secured Access Specifier is an uncommon sort of access specifier. When information part or part works are made secure, it also works to private and tends to be gotten to individuals from the class.

Kinds of Abstraction

There are two sorts of Abstraction:

1. Data Abstraction

2. Control Abstraction

Benefits of Abstraction

- No one but you can make changes to your information or work, and nobody else can.

- It makes the application secure by not permitting any other individual to see the foundation subtleties.

- Expands reusability of the code.

- Keeps away from duplication of your code.

Source Code:

```
#include<iostream>
using namespace std;
class test
{
```

```
private:
int x;
public:
test(int a)
{
x =a;
}
int get()
{
return x;
}
};
int main()
{
test a(5);
cout<<"Number is: "<<a.get();
return 0;
}
```

Output:

```
Number is: 5
```

HOW TO IMPLEMENT COPY CONSTRUCTOR IN C++?

Understanding Constructors has been a riddle for some. This article will assist you with demystifying the idea of Copy Constructor in C++. Following pointers will be canvassed in this article:

- Copy Constructor

- Shallow Copy Constructor

- Deep Copy Constructor

A Copy Constructor is a Constructor which introduces an object of a class utilizing one more object of a similar class.

We have the keyword const because we need to make the worth steady and ensure that it isn't altered in the code. Like a default constructor, a duplicate constructor is likewise given by the compiler. This is called Default Copy Constructor. Copy constructors can be made private. We can't duplicate the objects of the class when we make the duplicate constructor private.

Source Code:

```
#include<iostream>
using namespace std;
class test1
{
private:
int a;
public:
test(int a1)
{
a = a1;
}
test1(const test1 &c2)
{
x = c2.a;
}
int getB()
{
return a;
}
};
```

```
int main()
{
test c1(6); // Normal constructor is
called here
test c2 = c1; // Copy constructor is
called here
cout << "c1.a = " << c1.getB();
cout << "nc2.x = " << c2.getB();
return 0;
}
```

Output:

```
c1.a = 6
c2.a = 6
```

DATA HIDING

Data hiding is a platform developed for hiding internal object information, such as data members, in object-oriented programming. Data hiding ensures confined information admittance to class individuals and keeps up with object uprightness. In this blog, we will see how information concealing functions in C++.

- Encapsulation

- Abstraction

- Data Hiding

Encapsulation, abstraction & data hiding is firmly identified with one another. At the point when we talk about any C++ program, it comprises of two major components:

- Program explanations
- Program information

Encapsulation

Encapsulation ties the information and capacities together, which keeps the two safes from the outside impedance. Information epitome prompted statement stowing away.

Source Code:

```
#include<iostream>
using namespace std;
class Encap
{
    private:
        // data hidden from outside
        world
        int number;
    public:
        // function to set value of
        // variable a
        void set(int x)
        {
            number =x;
        }
        // function to return value of
        // variable a
        int get()
        {
            return number;
        }
};
// main function
```

```cpp
int main()
{
    Encap object;
    object.set(3);
    cout<<object.get();
    return 0;
}
```

Output:

3

Abstraction

Data Abstraction is an instrument of concealing the execution from the client and uncovering the interface.

Source Code:

```cpp
#include <iostream>
using namespace std;
class Abstraction
{
    private:
        int number1, number2;
    public:
        void set(int x, int y)
        {
            number1 = x;
            number2 = y;
        }
        void display()
        {
            cout<<"number1 = " <<number1
            << endl;
```

```
            cout<<"number2 = " <<
            number2 << endl;
        }
};

int main()
{
    Abstraction obj;
    obj.set(20, 50);
    obj.display();
    return 0;
}
```

Output:

```
number1 = 20
number2 = 50
```

Data Hiding

Data Hiding is a course of joining information and capacities into a solitary unit. The philosophy behind statement stowing away is to cover information inside a class, to keep its immediate access from outside the class. It assists software engineers in making classes with unique informational indexes and capacities, keeping away from extra infiltration from other program classes.

Talking about Data Hiding and information embodiment, information concealing shrouds class information parts, though information epitome shrouds class information parts and private strategies.

Presently you likewise need to know the entrance specifier for understanding information stowing away.

Private, public, and protected are three kinds of security/access specifiers accessible inside a class. Generally, the information inside a class is private and the capacities are public. The information is covered up with the goal that it will be protected from unintentional control.

Private individuals/techniques must be gotten to by strategies characterized as a component of the class. Information is regularly characterized as private to keep direct external access from different classes. Private individuals can be gotten to by individuals from the class.

Public individuals/techniques can be gotten to from any place in the program. Class techniques are generally open, which is utilized to control the information present in the class. When in doubt, information ought not to be proclaimed publicly. Public individuals can be gotten to by individuals and objects of the class.

Protected members are private inside a class and are accessible for private access in the determined class.

Source Code:

```
#include<iostream>
using namespace std;
class Base1{

    int number;   //by default private
    public:

    void read();
    void print();
};

void Base1 :: read(){
    cout<<"Enter value"<<endl;
    cin>>number;
```

```
}
void Base1 :: print(){
    cout<<"Value is "<<number<<endl;
}
int main(){
    Base1 object;
    object.read();
    object.print();

    return 0;
}
```

Output:

```
Enter value 5
Value is 5
```

IN C++, HOW DO YOU IMPLEMENT CONSTRUCTORS AND DESTRUCTORS?

C++ can undoubtedly be one of the main programming languages, on the off chance that you ask the current programming world. One of the many explanations behind it is the provisions it offers. This article will talk about one such element that is the constructor and destructor in C++.

- Constructor
- Default Constructor
- Parameterized Constructor
- Copy Constructor
- Destructor
- Virtual Destructor

Constructors and Destructors in C++

Constructor

A Constructor is a part capacity of a class. It is mostly used to introduce the objects of the class. It has a similar name as the class. The function Object is naturally referred to when an object is created. It's a unique kind of component capacity for a class.

The distinction between Constructor and other Member Functions:

1. The Constructor has a similar name as the class name.

2. The Constructor is considered when an object of the class is made.

3. A Constructor doesn't have a bring type back.

4. When a constructor isn't indicated, the compiler produces a default constructor that sits idle.

5. There are three kinds of constructors:

   i.   Default Constructor

   ii. Parameterized Constructor

   iii. Copy constructor

A constructor can likewise be characterized in the private segment of a class.

Default Constructor

A default constructor is a sort of constructor that doesn't take any contention and has no parameters.

Source Code:

```
#include <iostream>
using namespace std;
class test {
public:
int y, z;
test()
{
y = 8;
z = 11;
}
};
int main()
{
test a;
cout <<"the sum is: "<< a.y+a.z;
return 1;
}
```

Output:

```
19
```

Parameterized Constructor

The passing of parameters to the constructor is conceivable. This is done to introduce the worth of utilizing these passed boundaries. This kind of constructor is known as a Parameterized constructor.

The constructor is characterized as follows:

```
test(int x2)
{
x = x2;
}
```

There is a parameter that is passed to the constructor. The worth is passed when the article is made in principle work as displayed beneath.

```
test c(20);
```

Inside the fundamental capacity, we make an object of class test and pass the worth of the variable.

Source Code:

```
include <iostream>
using namespace std;
class test {
public:
int a;
test(int a1)
{
a = a1;
}
int getB()
{
return a;
}
};
int main()
{
test c(20);
cout << "b.a = " << b.getB();
return 0;
}
```

Output:

```
b.a = 20
```

Copy Constructor

A Copy Constructor is a Constructor which introduces an object of a class utilizing one more object of a similar class.

Source Code:

```
#include<iostream>
using namespace std;
class test1
{
private:
int a;
public:
test(int a1)
{
a = a1;
}
test(const test &c2)
{
x = c2.x;
}
int getB()
{
return a;
}
};
int main()
{
test c1(5); // Normal constructor is
called here
test c2 = c1; // Copy constructor is
called here
cout << "c1.a = " << c1.getB();
cout << "nc2.a = " << tc2.getB();
```

```
return 0;
}
```

Output:

```
c1.x = 5
c2.x = 5
```

Destructor

Destructors are one more sort of part work that is answerable for obliterating or erasing the item. It opens up space involved by the item after it is at this point not required. A Destructor is called naturally when the article is out of extension and as of now not required. A Destructor has the name same as the class name, however, the lone distinction is that the name is gone before by a tile ~.

Syntax:

```
~test1
```

There must be just a single Destructor in a class. A Destructor has no return type and no boundaries. On the off chance that we do indicate a destructor in class, the compiler makes a default destructor. The default destructor works fine except if memory is progressively dispensed or the pointer is proclaimed in the class.

The Destructor is called when:

- Function closes
- Program close

- A delete operator is called in the program.

- Block that contains the local variable finishes

Source Code:

```
#include <iostream>
using namespace std;
class test1 {
public:
int a, b;
test1()
{
a = 5;
b = 10;
}
~test1(){ }
};
int main()
{
test x;
cout <<"the sum is: "<< x.a+x.b;
return 1;
}
```

Output:

```
15
```

Virtual Destructor

The lone variety to the destructor is making the destructor virtual. This is done when we have an inheritance. During inheritance, the typical destructor acts vaguely. To fix this issue, the base class destructor must be announced as virtual.

```
class base1 {
public:
base1()
{ cout<<"Base Constructor n"; }
virtual ~base1()
{ cout<<"Base Destructor"; }
};
```

BASIC INPUT/OUTPUT IN C++

The C++ standard libraries offer a wide range of input/output capabilities, as we'll explore in the next chapters. This chapter will cover the most fundamental and often used I/O operations in C++ programming.

I/O in C++ happens in streams, which are byte sequences. The flow of bytes from a device such as a keyboard, a disc drive, or a network connection to main memory is known as input, while the flow of bytes from main memory to a device such as a display screen, a printer, a disc drive, or a network connection is known as output.

Header Files for the I/O Library

The following header files are required for a C++ program:

Sr. No	Header File & Function
1	**<iostream>**
	The cin, cout, cerr, and clog objects are defined in this file, and they correspond to the standard input stream, standard output stream, un-buffered standard error stream, and buffered standard error stream, respectively.

(Continued)

Sr. No	Header File & Function
2	**<iomanip>** This file specifies services that may be used to conduct formatted I/O using parameterized stream manipulators like setw and setprecision.
3	**<fstream>** This file defines user-controlled file processing services.

(cout) The Standard Output Stream

The ostream class is represented by the predefined object cout. The standard output device, which is generally the display screen, is said to be "attached to" the cout object. As demonstrated in the following example, the cout is combined with the stream insertion operator, which is represented as two less than signs.

Example:

```
#include <iostream>

using namespace std;

int main() {
    char str[] = "Hi everyone";

    cout << "The value of str: " << str
    << endl;
}
```

When the preceding code is built and run, the following result is obtained:

```
The value of str: Hi Everyone
```

In addition, the C++ compiler identifies the data type of the variable to be printed and chooses the proper stream insertion operator to show the value. To produce data items of built-in types integer, float, double, strings, and pointer values, the operator is overloaded.

As demonstrated above, the insertion operator can be used many times in a single statement, while endl is used to add a new line at the end of the line.

(cin) The Standard Input Stream

The istream class is represented by the predefined object cin. The conventional input device, which is generally the keyboard, is associated with the cin object. As demonstrated in the following example, the cin is used in conjunction with the stream extraction operator, which is represented as >>, which is two greater than signs.

Example:

```
#include <iostream>

using namespace std;

int main() {
    char n[30];

    cout << "Enter your name: ";
    cin >> n;
    cout << "Your name: " << n << endl;
}
```

When you compile and run the code above, it will request you for a name. To see the following result, you enter a value and then press enter.

```
Enter your name: cp
Your name: cp
```

The C++ compiler additionally identifies the data type of the input value and uses the appropriate stream extraction operation to extract and store the value in the variables.

(cerr) The Standard Error Stream

The ostream class has a preset object called cerr. The cerr object is claimed to be attached to the standard error device, which is also a display screen, but the object cerr is unbuffered, and each stream insertion causes cerr's output to show instantly.

As illustrated in the following example, the cerr can also be used with the stream insertion operator.

Example:

```cpp
#include <iostream>
using namespace std;
int main() {
    char str[] = "Un-able to read";
    cerr << "Error: " << str << endl;
}
```

When the given code is built and run, the following result is obtained:

```
Error: Un-able to read
```

(clog) The Standard Log Stream

The ostream class has a preset object called clog. The standard error device, which is also a display screen, is associated with the clog object, which is buffered. This implies that each addition to clog may result in the output being kept in a buffer until the buffer is full or flushed.

As illustrated in the following example, the clog may also be used with the stream insertion operator.

Example:

```
#include <iostream>
using namespace std;
int main() {
    char str[] = "Un-able to read";
    clog << "Error: " << str << endl;
}
```

When the preceding code is built and run, the following is the result:

```
Error: Un-able to read
```

With these short examples, you wouldn't be able to see the difference between cout, cerr, and clog, but the distinction becomes evident when developing and executing large programs. So, while displaying error messages, cerr stream should be utilized, and when displaying other log messages, clog should be used.

C++ DATA STRUCTURES

Structure is a user-defined data type that enables you to combine data items of different types. C/C++ arrays allow you to construct variables that mix many data items of the same kind, while structure is another user-defined data type that allows you to combine data items of other kinds.

Structures are used to represent a record. For example, let's say you want to keep track of your library books.

You may wish to keep note of the following characteristics for each book.

- Title

- Author

- Subject

- Book-id

Structure Defining

The struct statement is used to define a structure. The struct command creates a new data type for your application with many members. The struct statement has the following format:

Syntax:

```
struct [struc tag] {
   member definition;
   ....
   member definition;
};
```

Each member definition is a regular variable definition, such as int c float d; or any other acceptable variable definition, and the structure tag is optional. You can specify one or more structure variables before the last semicolon at the conclusion of the structure declaration, although this is optional. Here's how you'd go about declaring the Book structure:

Example:

```
struct books {
    char title[70];
    char author[60];
    char subject[90];
    int  book_id;
} book;
```

Using the Member to Access Structure Members

The member access operator is used to access any member of a structure (.). The member access operator is a period between the name of the structure variable and the name of the structure member we want to access. The struct keyword is used to define variables of the structure type. The following is an example of how to use structure:

Example:

```
#include <iostream>
#include <cstring>

using namespace std;

struct books {
    char  title[70];
    char  author[60];
    char  subject[90];
    int   book_id;
};

int main() {
    struct books book1;          //
    Declare Book1 of type Book
```

```cpp
struct books book2;          //
Declare Book2 of type Book
// specification of book 1
strcpy( book1.title, " C++
Programming");
strcpy( book1.author, "Chandi ");
strcpy( book1.subject, "C++ ");
book1.book_id = 64407;
// book 2 specification
strcpy( book2.title, " Billi");
strcpy( book2.author, "hakita");
strcpy( book2.subject, "Tele");
book2.book_id = 64700;

// Print
cout << "Booktitle : " << book1.
title <<endl;
cout << "Bookauthor : " << book1.
author <<endl;
cout << "Booksubject : " << book1.
subject <<endl;
cout << "Bookid : " << book1.book_id
<<endl;

// Print
cout << "Booktitle : " << book2.
title <<endl;
cout << "Bookauthor : " << book2.
author <<endl;
cout << "Booksubject : " << book2.
subject <<endl;
cout << "Bookid : " << book2.book_id
<<endl;
return 0;
}
```

Output:

```
Booktitle :  C++ Programming
Bookauthor : Chandi
Booksubject : C++
Bookid : 64407
Booktitle :  Billi
Bookauthor : hakita
Booksubject : Tele
Bookid : 64700
```

Structures as Function Arguments

A structure can be passed as a function parameter like any other variable or pointer can. Structure variables are accessible in the same way as variables in the previous example:

```cpp
#include <iostream>
#include <cstring>

using namespace std;
void printbook( struct books book );

struct books {
   char   title[70];
   char   author[60];
   char   subject[90];
   int    book_id;
};

int main() {
   struct books book1;        // Declare
   Book1 of type Book
   struct books book2;        // Declare
   Book2 of type Book
```

```cpp
   // specification of book 1
   strcpy( book1.title, " C++ Programming");
   strcpy( book1.author, "Chandi ");
   strcpy( book1.subject, "C++ ");
   book1.book_id = 64407;

   // book 2 specification
   strcpy( book2.title, " Billi");
   strcpy( book2.author, "hakita");
   strcpy( book2.subject, "Tele");
   book2.book_id = 64700;

   // Print book1info
   printbook( book1 );

   // Print book2 info
   printbook( book2 );

   return 0;
}
void printbook( struct books book ) {
   cout << "Booktitle : " << book.title
   <<endl;
   cout << "Bookauthor : " << book.author
   <<endl;
   cout << "Booksubject : " << book.subject
   <<endl;
   cout << "Bookid : " << book.book_id
   <<endl;
}
```

Output:

```
Booktitle : C++ Programming
Bookauthor : Chandi
```

```
Booksubject : C++
Bookid : 64407
Booktitle : Billi
Bookauthor : hakita
Booksubject : Tele
Bookid : 64700
```

This chapter covers the fundamentals of C++ syntax, as well as how to compile and run programs. What are the fundamental terminology of C++, such as semicolons, blocks, and keywords, and comments. We also learn about various sorts of data and variables and how to use several examples to illustrate types. Furthermore, what are Constants and Modifiers and their many types, as well as storage class, operators, and the various types of Loop and Decision statements.

We also touched upon topics such as what is a function in C++, and how do you declare one? What are arguments and what are Numbers, Arrays, Strings, and Pointers? Finally, using various words and examples, we learn how to take care of Files in C++.

CHAPTER 3

Working With Numbers and Spaces

IN THIS CHAPTER

➢ Converting between Numeric and String Types

➢ Limits and Other Properties of Numeric Types

➢ Creating Cooked and Raw User-defined Literals

➢ Building a Library of String Helpers

➢ Formatting Text with std::format

In the previous chapter, we learn about the basics of C++ syntax and how to build and run programs, which are covered in the preceding chapter. What is the basic C++

DOI: 10.1201/9781003214762-3

vocabulary, such as semicolons, blocks, keywords, and comments? We also learn about different types of data and variables and how to utilize a variety of examples to demonstrate them. What are Constants and Modifiers, and the various forms of storage classes, operators, and the numerous sorts of Loop and Decision statements? What exactly is a C++ function, and how do you declare one? What are the differences between arguments and Numbers, Arrays, Strings, and Pointers? Finally, we learned how to take care of Files in C++ using various terms and examples.

In this chapter, we will focus on working with different number types and strings.

CHANGING NUMERIC TYPES TO STRING TYPES

When creating C++ programs, it is usual to convert strings to numbers such as integers and doubles. This section discusses the functions that may convert strings to int and double values and numeric values to strings. When we use C++ to create programs, we must transform data from one type to another. Data conversion should be done so that no data is lost when existing data is converted to a new kind. This is especially true when converting textual data to integers and the other way around.

Changing a String to a Number

- **Method 1:** Using the stringstream or sscanf classes ().

- **Method 2:** Using stoi() or atoi to convert strings ().

- Both of these techniques have been thoroughly explored.

- Boost lexical cast is the third method.

The Boost library has a built-in function called lexical cast("string") that transforms a string into a number. If the input is invalid, it throws the "bad lexical cast" exception.

Using stoi and atoi the std::string class provides several methods for converting strings to integers, longs, doubles, floats, and other types. std:: supports the following conversion functions. The following is a table of the strings:

Function	Description
stoi stol stoll	A string is converted to an integer using this method.
atoi atol atoll	A byte string is converted to an integer using this method.
stod stof stold	Floating-point values are transformed from bytes.
stoul stoull	A byte string is converted to an unsigned integer using this method.

Example:

```
//C++ code to demonstrate working of
lexical_cast()

#include<iostream>
#include <boost/lexical_cast.hpp>
#include <string> // for string
using namespace std;
int main()
{
string str = "4";
string str1 = "4.5";
```

```cpp
// Initializing f_value with casted float
// f_value is 4.5
float f_value = boost::lexical_cast
<float>(str1);

// Initializing i_value with casted int
// i_value is 5
int i_value = boost::lexical_cast<int>
(str);

//Displaying casted values
cout << "The float value after casting : ";
cout << f_value <<endl;
cout << "The int value after casting : ";
cout << i_value <<endl;

return 0;
}
```

Output:

```
The float value after casting: 4.5
The int value after casting: 4
```

Changing a Number to a String

The First Method Is to Use String Streams

String stream defines a stream object in this function, which enters a number as a stream into the object and then uses "str()" to convert the number to a string internally.

Example:

```cpp
// C++ code to demonstrate string
stream method
// to convert number to string.
#include<iostream>
```

```cpp
#include <sstream> // for string
streams
#include <string> // for string
using namespace std;
int main()
{
    int num = 2020;

    // declaring output string stream
    ostringstream str1;

    // Sending a number as a stream
into output
    // string
    str1 << num;

    // the str() converts number into
string
    string geek = str1.str();

    // Displaying the string
    cout << "Newly formed string from
number is : ";
    cout << gone<< endl;

    return 0;
}
```

Output:

```
Newly formed string from number: 2020
```

The Second Method Is Used to String Function ()
This method takes a number (of any data type) and returns it as a string.

Example:

```
// C++ code to demonstrate "to_string()"
method
// to convert number to string.
#include<iostream>
#include<string> // for string and
to_string()
using namespace std;
int main()
{
    // Declaring integer
    int i_val = 10;

    // Declaring float
    float f_val = 20.50;

    // Conversion of int into string
using
    // to_string()
    string stri = to_string(i_val);

    // Conversion of float into string
using
    // to_string()
    string strf = to_string(f_val);

    // Displaying the converted strings
    cout << "The integer in string: ";
    cout << stri << endl;
    cout << "The float in string: ";
    cout << strf << endl;

    return 0;
}
```

Output:

```
The integer in string: 10
The float in string: 20.500000
```

The Third Method Is Used to Boost Lexical Cast

The "lexical cast()" method is similar to string conversion, except the parameter list is changed to "lexical cast(numeric var)".

Example:

```
// C++ code to demonstrate "lexical_
cast()" method
// to convert number to string.
#include <boost/lexical_cast.hpp> //
for lexical_cast()
#include <string> // for string
using namespace std;
int main()
{
// Declaring float
float f_val = 8.5;

// Declaring int
int i_val = 14;

// lexical_cast() converts a float
into string
string strf = boost::lexical_cast
<string>(f_val);

// lexical_cast() converts a int into
string
```

```
string stri = boost::lexical_cast
<string>(i_val);

// Displaying string converted numbers
cout << "The float value in string: ";
cout << strf << endl;
cout << "The int value in string: ";
cout << stri << endl;

return 0;
}
```

Output:

```
The float value in string: 8.5
The int value in string: 14
```

Numbers are stored in database columns as numeric data types. Exact numeric types, values where must be keep accurate and scale are examples of these data types. INTEGER, BIGINT, DECIMAL, NUMERIC, NUMBER, and MONEY are the precise numeric kinds.

Variable Types and Limitations Are Standard

The following Tables 3.1 to 3.3 lists the integer types' limitations in C and C++. Limitations.h> is a C standard header file that defines certain limits. climits>, which contains limits.h>, is included in the C++ Standard Library header limits>.

Sized integer variables, which are integral types of size 8-, 16-, 32-, or 64-bits, may also be declared in Microsoft C. See Sized Integer Types for additional information on sized integers in C.

TABLE 3.1 Numeric Types

Type	Size (in bits)	Format	Minimum Value	Maximum Value	Literal Suffix	Sig. Digits
BYTE	8	Signed integer	−128	+127		2+
UBYTE	8	Unsigned integer	0	+255		2+
SHORT	16	Signed integer	−32,768	+32,767		4+
USHORT	16	Unsigned integer	0	65,535		4+
INTEGER	32	Signed integer	−2,147,483,648	+2,147,483,647	%, l	9+
UINTEGER	32	Unsigned integer	0	4,294,967,295	ul	9+
LONG	[*]	Signed integer	[*]	[*]	&	[*]
ULONG	[*]	Unsigned integer	[*]	[*]		[*]
LONGINT	64	Signed integer	−9,223,372,036,854,775,808	+9,223,372,036,854,775,807	ll	18+
ULONGINT	64	Unsigned integer	0	+18,446,744,073,709,551,615	ull	19+
SINGLE	32	Floating point	[**]+/−1.401 298 E−45	[**]+/−3.402 823 E+38	!, f	6+
DOUBLE	64	Floating point	[**]+/−4.940 656 458 412 465 E−324	[**]+/−1.797 693 134 862 316 E+308	#	15+

TABLE 3.2   String Types

Type	Character Size (in bytes)	Minimum Size (in characters)	Maximum Size (in characters)	Literal Suffix
String	1	0	[**]+2,147,483,647	$
Zstring	1	0	[**]+2,147,483,647	[N/A]
Wstring	[*]	[*]0	[*,**]+2,147,483,647	[N/A]

TABLE 3.3   Arrays

Maximum Subscript Range	Maximum Elements per Dimension	Minimum/ Maximum Dimensions	Maximum Size (in bytes)
[*][−2,147,483,648, +2,147,483,647]	[*]+2,147,483,647	1/9	[*]+2,147,483,647

C++ NUMERIC DATA TYPES

C++ is a fundamental programming language that unusually uses numeric data types. Integers and floating points are two different kinds of numeric data. Whole numbers are integers, while decimal points are floating points.

Types of Primitive Data

These data types are built-in or preset data types that may be used to declare variables directly by the user.

- Integer

- Character

- Boolean

- Floating Point

- Double Floating Point

- Valueless or Void
- Wide Character

Derived Data Types

Derived Data Types are information types that are gotten from crude or underlying data types. They are separated into four classifications:

1. Function

2. Array

3. Pointer

4. Reference

User-Defined Data Types

These are data types that the user defines. As an example, in C++, declaring a class or a structure. The following user-defined datatypes are available in C++:

- Class

- Structure

- Union

- Enumeration

- Typedef defined DataType

C++ Provides the Following Primitive Data Types

- **Integer:** Integer data types are described by the keyword int. Integers have a range of –2,147,483,648 to 2,147,483,647 and take up 4 bytes of memory.

- **Character:** Characters are stored using the data type character. The keyword for the character data type is char, and characters range from −128 to 127 or 0 to 255, taking up 1 byte of RAM on average.

- **Boolean:** True or false can be saved in a boolean variable, which uses the boolean data type to hold logical or boolean values. The keyword for the boolean data type is bool.

- **Floating Point:** The Floating Point data type stores floating point or decimal numbers with single precision. The keyword float is used to describe the floating-point data type. Float variables usually take up 4 bytes of memory.

- **Double Floating Point:** The Double Floating Point data type stores floating point or decimal numbers with double precision. The keyword double is used to describe the double floating-point data type. Double variables usually take up 8 bytes of memory.

- **Void:** The term void refers to something that has no worth. The void datatype represents a valueless entity.

User-Defined Literals' Objectives

Only the "interesting" categories of literals can have user-defined literals: integral numbers, floating-point numbers, characters, and character strings. New literal types can be defined (it is not possible to specify new literal prefixes). As stated in the proposals, the Committee's primary aims were to provide a mechanism for describing new literal types using the Standard Library rather than expanding the core language. It looks that changing the Standard Library is less complicated. The Committee intends to utilize this tool to add any literals introduced to C or standard C extensions or planned to be added in the future. A decimal floating-point literal, such as 10.2df, is one such example. Because many new C literals require prefixes or syntax other than suffixes/prefixes, this aim has only been partially met:

- binary integer literals (0b11011) (offered to C but refused)

- 0x102Ap12 is a hex floating-point literal

- u'A' is a new char literal

The literals also served as a springboard for developing additional C++ Standard Library components such as arbitrary-precision integers, decimal floating-point numbers, fixed-point numbers, new string types, and SI units.

While user-defined literals are primarily a tool for Standard Library designers, they are also available to ordinary users with restrictions.

Integers

In programming, integers are classified into three categories: short int, int, and long int. A short int can be any integer between –32,768 and 32,767, but a regular int, sometimes known as just int, has a much more extensive range, ranging from 2,147,483,648 to 2,147,483,647.

It's crucial to remember that in C++, there's no one standard for numeric data types. Thus the names and range values may change somewhat depending on the implementation and processor.

Example

```
out << 'short int Min/Max : ' << SHRT_
MIN << ' / ' << SHRT_MAX << endl;
cout << 'int Min/Max : ' << INT_MIN <<
' / ' << INT_MAX << endl;
cout << 'long Min/Max : ' << LONG_MIN
<< ' / ' << LONG_MAX << endl;
```

Decimal

The decimal data type is a very exact numeric data type distinguished by its accuracy and scale.

Floating Points

The second category of numeric data types in C++ is floats. As the name indicates, floating points can have a decimal, providing them a higher level of precision than integers.

In C++, floating-point numbers are divided into three categories: float, double, and long double. Floats are the smallest, followed by images, which are twice the size of doubles, and long doubles, which are twice the size of long doubles. The code below will provide an output that shows the float data types' lowest and maximum values.

Example

```
cout << '\tFloat \t\t' << 'Double \t\t'
<< 'Long Double' << endl;
cout << 'Min : ' << FLT_MIN << '\t' <<
DBL_MIN << '\t' << LDBL_MIN << endl;
```

```cpp
cout << 'Max : ' << FLT_MAX << '\t' <<
DBL_MAX << '\t' << LDBL_MAX << endl;
```

LITERALS SPECIFIED BY THE USER

The C++ language has several built-in literals (numerical, character, string, boolean, and pointer) as well as a set of prefixes and suffixes that may be used to designate them. The literal includes the suffix or prefix.

Example:

```cpp
auto b = true;      // boolean
auto s = "sam"; // const char[7]
auto i = 18;        // int
auto d = 18.0;      // double

// with prefixes
auto w = L"Hello";  // const wchar_t[5]
auto h = 0xBAD;     // int (in
hexadecimal representation)

// with suffixes
auto a = 18u;       // unsigned int
auto l = 18l;       // signed long
auto f = 18.0f;     // float
```

The C++11 standard included the ability to construct user-defined literals, which are built-in type literals (integer, float, char, or string) with a user-defined suffix. User-defined literals allow you to create new objects using the built-in literal value plus a user-defined suffix.

```cpp
auto temp = 77_fah;
auto size = 1_KB;
auto emp = "marius"_dev;
```

COOKED

The literal 0xBAD is "0", "x", "B", "A", "D" in raw form and a compiler-interpreted type of characters; the literal 0xBAD is the integer 2898 in cooked form.

Literals Specified by the User

- Only the suffix form is supported; it is not feasible to define prefixes;

- Begin with an underscore ('_'); the standard reserves all suffixes that begin with any other character than an underscore.

- It may be used both raw and cooked; Strings that can only expand in the cooked form reflect the exception.

Cooked Literals

For a cooked literal, the literal operator has the following form:

Example

```
OutputType operator "" _suffix(InputType);
```

Only a few forms of input are permitted

The type is unsigned long long for integral literals (decimal, octal, hexadecimal, or binary)

Example:

```
OutputType operator "" _suffix(unsigned
long long);
```

The type for floating-point types is long double

Example:

```
OutputType operator "" _suffix(long
double);
```

Sorts for characters:

Example

```
OutputType operator "" _suffix(char);
OutputType operator "" _suffix
(wchar_t);
OutputType operator "" _suffix
(char16_t);
OutputType operator "" _suffix
(char32_t);
```

LITERALS OF RAW

Only integral and floating-point types support raw literals. The literal operator for a cooked literal is as follows (note that the operator does not take a second parameter to specify the size of the string; the string is null-terminated):

```
OutputType operator "" _suffix(const char*);
```

To parse this array of characters, you can use loops, variable definitions, function calls, and other approaches. Consequently, this type of literal operator can't be constexpr, which means can't evaluate it at compile time.

A literal operator variadic template is another option for processing raw literals. A variadic template literal operator's goal is to do the literal translation at compile time. The literal operator template has the following format:

```
template<char...> OutputType operator ""
_tuffix();
```

Consider the following example, in which we define a 4 KB buffer:

```
std::array<unsigned char, 4_KB> buffer;
```

This is the same as the following statement:

```
std::array<unsigned char, 4096> buffer;
```

The size of the array should be specified at compile-time, and the compiler would throw an error while declaring the buffer variable if the literal operator was not a constexpr. The user-defined literal would still be used in runtime circumstances, such as when scaling a vector.

```
std::vector<unsigned char> buffer(4_KB);
```

The literal operator's return type can be any type; unlike the preceding examples, it does not have a built-in type. We may construct user-defined literals that enable the development of developer and quality assurer objects using the following hierarchy of classes:

Example

```
class Emp
{
    std::string name;
```

```cpp
public:
   Emp(std::string const & name)
:name(name){}
   std::string getName() const { return
name; }
};

class Dev : public Emp
{
public:
   using Emp::Emp;
};

class QualityAssurer : public Emp
{
public:
   using Emp::Emp;
};

Dev op "" _dev(char const * text,
std::size_t const size)
{
   return Dev(std::string(text, text +
size));
}

QualAss op "" _qa(char const * text,
std::size_t const size)
{
   return QualAss(std::string(text,
text + size));
}

int main()
{
```

```
    auto e = "mari"_dev;
    auto d = "Tia"_qa;
    std::cout << d.getName() << std::endl;
    std::cout << q.getName() << std::endl;

    return 0;
}
```

STANDARD USER-DEFINED LITERALS

Several literal operators are defined in C++14:

- For constructing a std::complex, use the operators""if, operator""i, and operator""il.

    Example:

    ```
    #include <complex>

    int main()
    {
       using namespace
    std::literals::complex_literals;
       std::complex<double> c = 1.0 + i;
    }
    ```

- operator""min, operator""s, operator""us, operator""h for creating a std::chrono::duration value.

    Example

    ```
    #include <chrono>
    int main()
    {
    ```

```
    using namespace
std::literals::chrono_literals;
    auto timer = 2h + 20min + 20s;
}
```

- For converting a character array literal to a std::basic_ string, use the operator""s.

Example

```
int main()
{
    using namespace
std::string_literals;
    std::string d1 = "text\0";  // d1
= "text"
    std::string d2 = "text\0"s; // d2
= "text\0"
}
```

STRING HELPER

The String Helper file includes methods to help with string manipulation.

- Loading this Helper
- Available Functions

The following code is used to load this helper:

Syntax:

```
$this->load->helper('string');
```

Functions that is available:

There are the following functions available:

Syntax:

```
random_string([$type = 'alnum'[, $len
= 8]])
```

Parameters:

- **$type (string):** Randomization type

- **$len (int):** Output string length

Returns: A random string
Return type: string

The type and length you give are used to generate a random string. It may be used to create passwords or generate random hashes.

The first argument determines the string's type, while the second specifies its length. There are multiple options available:

- **alpha:** A string consisting solely of lower and capital characters.

- **alnum:** An alphanumeric string that includes lowercase and uppercase characters.

- **basic:** mt rand-based random number ().

- **numeric:** A string of numbers.

- **nozero:** nozero is a numeric string that contains no zeros.

- **md5:** An md5()-based encrypted random number (fixed length of 32).

- **sha1:** sha1() generates an encrypted random number (fixed length of 40).

Example:

```
echo random_string('alnum', 26);
```

- increment_string($str[, $separator = '_'[, $second = 2]])

Parameters:

- **$str (string):** String to be entered

- **$separator (string):** Append a duplicate number with a separator

- **$first (int):** Number to begin with

Returns: a string that has been increased in length
Return type: string

Append a number to a string or increase the number to increment it. Creating "copies" of a file or replicating database information with distinct titles or slugs is a breeze with this tool.

Example:

```
echo increment_string('file', '_'); //
echo increment_string('file', '-', 3);
echo increment_string('file_5');
```

- alternator($args)

Parameters:

- **$args (mixed):** The number of parameters is vary.

Returns: Alternated string
Return type: mixed

When cycling through a loop, this feature allows you to alternate between two or more objects.

Example:

```
for ($i = 0; $i < 10; $i++)
{
        echo alternator('string one',
'string two');
}
```

You may add as many arguments as you wish, and the next item will be returned after each iteration of your loop.

Example:

```
for ($i = 0; $i < 10; $i++)
{
        echo alternator('one', 'two',
'three', 'four', 'five');
}
```

- repeater($data[, $num = 1])

Parameters:

- **$data (string):** Input

- **$num (int):** The number of times you should repeat it

Returns: Repeated string
Return type: string

Repeating copies of the data you enter are generated

Example:

```
$string = "\n";
echo repeater($string, 30);
```

- reduce_double_slashes($str)

Parameters: $str (string)—String to be entered
Returns: Slashes that have been normalized in a string
Return type: string

Except for those present in URL protocol prefixes (e.g. http://), converts double slashes in a text to a single slash

Example:

```
$string = "http://example.com//index.
php";
echo reduce_double_slashes($string);
```

- strip_slashes($data)

Parameters: $data—String to be entered
Returns: stripped slashes with string
Type of return: mixed

Slashes are removed from a string array

Example:

```
$str = array(
        'question'  => 'your name O\
illy?',
        'answer' => ' my name is
O\'nnor.'
);
$str = strip_slashes($str);
```

- trim_slashes($str)

Parameters: $str (string)—Input string
Returns: Slash-trimmed string
Type of return: string

Removes the string's leading and trailing slashes

Example:

```
$string = "/this/that/theother/";
echo trim_slashes($string);
```

- reduce_multiples($str[, $character = "[, $trim = FALSE]])

Parameters:

- **$str (string):** Text to look for

- **$character (string):** Reduced character

- **$trim (bool):** Whether the supplied character should additionally be trimmed

Returns: Reduced string length
Type of return: string

Reduces the number of times a character appears immediately after another.

Example:

```
$string = "Fill, hill, Toe, Jim";
$string = reduce_multiples($string,",")
```

* quotes_to_entities($str)

Parameters: $str (string)—String to be entered
Returns: HTML entities converted from a string with quotations
Type of return: string

Needs to convert single and double quotes in a string to their corresponding HTML entities

Example:

```
$string = "Toe's \"food\"";
$string = quotes_to_entities($string);
```

* strip_quotes($str)

Parameters: $str (string)—Input string
Returns: String with quotes stripped
Type of return: string

Single and double quotes are removed from a string.

Example:

```
$string = "Toe's \"food\"";
$string = strip_quotes($string);
```

TEXT HELPER

This file includes routines that make dealing with text easier.

- Loading this Helper
- Available Functions

Loading This Helper

The following code is used to load this helper:

Syntax:

```
$this->load->helper('text');
```

Available Functions

The following functionalities are accessible:

- word_limiter($str[, $limit = 100[, $end_char = 'Ѫ']])

Parameters:

- **$str (string):** String to be entered
- **$limit (int):** Limit
- **$end_char (string):** Character's end

Returns: String with a word limit
Type of return: string

Reduces the length of a string to the specified amount of words

Example:

```
$string = " String consisting of eleven
words.";
$string = word_limiter($string, 5);
```

The third parameter is a string suffix that can be appended. It inserts an ellipsis by default

- character_limiter($str[, $n = 200[, $end_char = 'ᑮ']])

Parameters:

- **$str (string):** String to be entered

- **$n (int):** the total number of characters

- **$end_char (string):** Character's end

Returns: String with a character limit
Type of return: string

The character count may differ slightly from what you want since the string is truncated to the specified number of characters.

Example:

```
$string = "String consisting of eleven
words.";
$string = character_limiter($string, 20);
```

The third parameter is an optional string suffix; the helper uses an ellipsis if none is specified.

- ascii_to_entities($str)

Parameters: $str (string)—String to be entered

Returns: A string made up of ASCII values that have been converted into entities.

Type of return: string

Converts ASCII data to character entities, including high ASCII and MS Word characters that might create web page issues; it won't be perfect in every circumstance. Still, in the great majority of cases, it should distinguish characters outside of the standard range.

Example:

```
$string = ascii_to_entities($string);
```

- convert_accented_characters($str)

Parameters: $str (string)—to be entered string

Returns: Converting a string containing accented letters

Return type: string

High ASCII characters are converted to their low ASCII counterparts. This is useful when non-English characters must be used in places where only standard ASCII characters are safe, such as URLs.

Example:

```
$string =
convert_accented_characters($string);
```

- word_censor($str, $censored[, $replacement = "])

Parameters:

- **$str (string):** String to be entered

- **$censored (array):** List of terms that should be avoided

- **$replacement (string):** What should be used to replace bad words

Returns: Censored string
Return type: string

You may use this feature to censor terms inside a text string. The original string will be the first argument. The second will have a list of terms that you are not allowed to use. The third parameter can be used to specify a replacement value for the words. They are substituted with pound signs if they are not limited: ####.

Example:

```
$disallowed = array('darn', 'shucks',
'golly', 'phooey');
$string = word_censor($string,
$disallowed, 'Beep!');
```

- highlight_code($str)

Parameters: $str (string)—String to be entered
Returns: HTML-enabled string with code highlighted
Return type: string

Example:

```
$string = highlight_code($string);
```

TYPOGRAPHY ASSIST

The Typography Helper file includes routines that aid in the semantically appropriate formatting of text.

This helper is currently being loaded.

- Available Functions

- Loading this Helper

The following code is used to load this helper:

Example:

```
$this->load->helper('typography');
```

Available Functions

There are the following functions available:

- auto_typography($str[, $reduce_linebreaks = FALSE])

Parameters:

- **$str (string):** Input string

- **$reduce_linebreaks (bool):** Whether to reduce multiple instances of double newlines to two

Returns: HTML-formatted typography-safe string
Return type: string

Text is formatted in HTML to be semantically and typographically correct.

CI Typography::auto typography is an alias for this function (). Please read the Typography Library documentation for additional information.

Example:

```
$string = auto_typography($string);
```

- nl2br_except_pre($str)

Parameters: $str (string)—Input string
Returns: String with HTML-formatted line breaks
Return type: string

If newlines exist within pre> tags, they are converted to br /> tags. Except that it skips pre> tags, this method is similar to the native PHP nl2br() function.

Example:

```
$string = nl2br_except_pre($string);
```

- entity_decode($str, $charset = NULL)

Parameters:

- **$str (string):** Input string

- **$charset (string):** Character set

Returns: String with decoded HTML entities
Return type: string

CI Security::entity decode is an alias for this function ().

URL HELPER

The URL Helper file includes routines that make working with URLs easier.

This helper is currently being loaded

- Loading this Helper
- Available Functions

Loading This Helper

The following code is used to load this helper:

Syntax:

```
$this->load->helper('URL);
```

Available Functions

There are the following functions available:

- site_url([$uri = "[, $protocol = NULL]])

Parameters:

- **$uri (string):** URI string

- **$protocol (string):** Protocol, e.g. "http" or "https"

Returns: Site URL
Return type: string

Returns the URL of your site, as defined in your config file. Any URI segments you give to the function, as well as the URL suffix specified in your config file, will be appended to the URL, as will the index.php file (or whatever you select as your site index page in your config file).

This method should be used whenever you need to build a local URL to make your pages more portable if your URL changes.

Optionally, segments can be provided to the method as a string or an array.

Example:

```
echo site_url('news/local/123');
```

- base_url($uri = ", $protocol = NULL)

Parameters:

- **$uri (string):** URI string

- **$protocol (string):** Protocol, e.g. "http" or "https"

Returns: Base URL
Return type: string

Returns your site base URL, as specified in your config file.

Example:

```
echo base_url();
```

This function provides the same result as site URL(), but without the index page and URL suffix.

You can pass segments as a string or an array, much like site URL().

Example:

```
echo base url("blog/post/123");
```

- current_url()

Returns: The current URL
Return type: string

- uri_string()

Returns: An URI string
Return type: string

This method returns the URI segments of any page that contains it.

Example:

http://some-site.com/blog/comments/123

- index_page()

Returns: "index_page" value
Return type: mixed

Returns the index page for your site, as defined in your config file

Example:

```
echo index_page();
```

- anchor($uri = ", $title = ", $attributes = ")

Parameters:

- **$uri (string):** URI string

- **$title (string):** Anchor title

- **$attributes (mixed):** HTML attributes

Returns: HTML hyperlink (anchor tag)
Return type: string

Example:

```
echo anchor('news/local/123', 'News',
'title="Title"');
```

- anchor_popup($uri = ", $title = ", $attributes = FALSE)

Parameters:

- **$uri (string):** URI string

- **$title (string):** Anchor title

- **$attributes (mixed):** HTML attributes

Returns: Pop-up hyperlink
Return type: string

- mailto($email, $title = ", $attributes = ")

Parameters:

- **$email (string):** E-mail address

- **$title (string):** Anchor title

- **$attributes (mixed):** HTML attributes

Returns: A "mail to" hyperlink
Return type: string

Example:

```
echo mailto('me@my-site.com', 'Click
Here to Contact Me');
```

- safe_mailto($email, $title = ", $attributes = ")

Parameters:

- **$email (string):** E-mail address

- **$title (string):** Anchor title

- **$attributes (mixed):** HTML attributes

Returns: A spam-safe "mail to" hyperlink
Return type: string

- auto_link($str, $type = 'both', $popup = FALSE)

Parameters:

- **$str (string):** Input string

- **$type (string):** Link type ("email", "url", or "both")

- **$popup (bool):** Whether to create popup links

Returns: Linkified string
Return type: string

- url_title($str, $separator = '-', $lowercase = FALSE)

Parameters:

- **$str (string):** Input string

- **$separator (string):** Word separator

- **$lowercase (bool):** Whether to transform the output string to lower-case

Returns: URL-formatted string
Return type: string

Example:

```
$title = " CSS Problems?";
$url_title = url_title($title);
```

- prep_url($str = ")

Parameters: $str (string)—URL string
Returns: Protocol-prefixed URL string
Return type: string

- redirect($uri = ", $method = 'auto', $code = NULL)

Parameters:

- **$uri (string):** URI string

- **$method (string):** Redirect method ("auto", "location", or "refresh")

- **$code (string):** HTTP Response code (usually 302 or 303)

Return type: void

XML HELPER

The XML Helper file includes methods that make dealing with XML data easier.

- Loading this Assistant

- Functions available

Loading This Assistant

Functions available

This helper is currently being loaded.

Syntax:

```
$this->load->helper('xml');
```

Functions available

There are the following functions available:

- xml_convert($str[, $protect_all = FALSE])

Parameters:

- **$str (string):** the text string to be transformed

- **$protect_all (bool):** Whether all text that appears to be a possible entity, rather than numbered entities, such as &foo; should be protected.

Returns: string that has been translated to XML
Return type: string

Using a text as input converts the following reserved XML characters to entities:

- Ampersands: &

- Less than and more significant than characters: < >

- Single and double quotes: ' "

- Dashes: -

Example:

```
$string = '<p>Here is a paragraph & an
entity ({).</p>';
$string = xml_convert($string);
echo $string;
```

STD::STRING

C++ includes a method for representing a series of characters as a class object in its definition. std:: string is the name of this class. The String class holds characters as a series of bytes, with the ability to retrieve a single-byte character.

Character Array vs. std:: string:

- A character array is just a collection of characters that can end with a null character. A string is a type of object that may be represented as a continuous stream of characters.

- The size of the character array must be allocated statically; if extra memory is necessary, it cannot be allocated at run time. In the case of a character array, any allocated memory that is not used is squandered. Memory is allocated dynamically in the case of strings. On-demand, more memory can be assigned during runtime. There is no memory waste since no memory is preallocated.

- In the case of a character array, there is a risk of array decay. There is no array decay since strings are represented as objects.

- Character array implementation is quicker than std:: string implementation. When compared to character arrays, strings are slower to implement.

- There aren't many built-in functions for manipulating strings in character arrays. The String class offers several features that enable for a variety of string operations.

String Operations Include
Functions for Input

- **getline():** This function stores a stream of characters entered by the user in object memory.

- **push back():** Use this method to insert a character at the end of a string.

- **pop back():** This method was introduced in C++11(for strings) and is used to remove the final character from the string.

Example:

```cpp
// C++ code to demonstrate the working of
// getline(), push_back() and
pop_back()

#include<iostream>
#include<string>
using namespace std;
int main()
{
   // Declaring string
   string str;

   // Taking string input using
getline()
   // "helloeveryone" in giving output
   getline(cin,str);

   // Displaying string
   cout << "The initial string is : ";
   cout << str << endl;
```

```
    // Using push_back() to insert a
character
    // at end
    // pushes 's' in this case
    str.push_back('s');

    // Displaying string
    cout << "The string after push_back
operation is : ";
    cout << str << endl;

    // Using pop_back() to delete a
character
    // from end
    // pops 's' in this case
    str.pop_back();

    // Displaying string
    cout << "The string after pop_back
operation is : ";
    cout << str << endl;

    return 0;
}
```

Output:

```
The initial string is: helloeveryone
The string after push_back operation
is: helloeveryone
The string after pop_back operation
is: helloeveryone'
```

Functions of Capacity

- **capacity()**: This method returns the string's capacity, which can be equal to or more than the string's size. Additional space is set aside to complete actions quickly when additional characters are introduced to the string.

- **resize()**: This method alters the length of a string, allowing it to be increased or lowered.

- **length()**: This method returns the string's length.

- **shrink to fit()**: This function reduces the string's capacity until it is equal to the string's minimal capacity. If we are certain that no more character additions are required, we may utilize this method to conserve memory.

Example:

```
// C++ code to demonstrate the working
of
// capacity(), resize() and
shrink_to_fit()
#include<iostream>
#include<string> // for string class
using namespace std;
int main()
{
   // Initializing string
   string str = " helloeveryone is for
college ";
```

```
    // Displaying string
    cout << "Initial string: ";
    cout << str << endl;

    // Resizing string using resize()
    str.resize(13);

    // Displaying string
    cout << "String after resize
operation : ";
    cout << str << endl;

    // Displaying capacity of string
    cout << "Capacity of string: ";
    cout << str.capacity() << endl;

    //Displaying length of the string
    cout<<"Length of the string:"<<str.
length()<<endl;

    // Decreasing the capacity of string
    // using shrink_to_fit()
    str.shrink_to_fit();
    return 0;
}
```

Output:

```
Initial string: helloeveryone is for
college
String after resize operation:
helloeveryone
Capacity of string: 27
Length of the string:12
```

Iterator Methods

- **begin()**: This method returns an iterator to the first character in the string.

- **end()**: Returns an iterator to the end of the string.

- **rbegin()**: This method returns a reverse iterator that points to the string's end.

- **rend()**: This method produces a reverse iterator that points to the start of the string.

Example:

```
// C++ code to demonstrate the working of
// begin(), end(), rbegin(), rend()

#include<iostream>
#include<string> // for string class
using namespace std;
int main()
{
   // Initializing string`
   string str = "helloeveryone";

   // Declaring iterator
   std::string::iterator it;

   // Declaring reverse iterator
   std::string::reverse_iterator it1;

   // Displaying string
```

```
    cout << "String using forward
iterators: ";
    for (it=str.begin(); it!=str.end();
it++)
    cout << *it;
    cout << endl;

    // Displaying reverse string
    cout << "Reverse string using
reverse iterators: ";
    for (it1=str.rbegin(); it1!=str.
rend(); it1++)
    cout << *it1;
    cout << endl;

    return 0;
}
```

Output:

```
String using forward iterators:
helloeveryone
Reverse string using reverse iterators:
enoyreveolleh
```

Functions Manipulation

- **copy("char array", len, pos):** This method copies the substring from the destination character array specified in the parameters. It has three arguments: a target char array, a length to copy, and a starting point in the string to copy from.

- **swap():** switches one string with another.

Example:

```cpp
// C++ code to demonstrate the working of
// copy() and swap()
#include<iostream>
#include<string> // for string class
using namespace std;
int main()
{
    // Initializing 1st string
    string str1 = " everyone is for college ";

    // Declaring 2nd string
    string str2 = "everyone rocks";

    // Declaring character array
    char ch[80];

    // using copy() to copy elements into char array
    // copies "everyone"
    str1.copy(ch,13,0);

    // Displaying char array
    cout << "The new copied character array is : ";
    cout << ch << endl << endl;

    // Displaying strings before swapping
    cout << "The 1st string before swapping is : ";
```

```
   cout << str1 << endl;
   cout << "The 2nd string before
swapping is : ";
   cout << str2 << endl;

   // using swap() to swap string
content
   str1.swap(str2);

   // Displaying strings after swapping
   cout << "The 1st string after
swapping is : ";
   cout << str1 << endl;
   cout << "The 2nd string after
swapping is : ";
   cout << str2 << endl;

   return 0;

}
```

Output:

```
The new copied character array is:
everyone

The 1st string before swapping is:
everyone is for college
The 2nd string before swapping is:
everyone rocks
The 1st string after swapping is:
everyone rocks
The 2nd string after swapping is:
everyone is for college
```

LIBRARY FORMATTING

The text formatting library is a secure and flexible replacement for the printf routines. It's meant to work with the current C++ I/O streams library, reusing parts of its infrastructure like overloaded insertion operators for user-defined types.

Example:

```
std::string message = std::format("The
answer is {}.", 42);
```

Formatting options include:

format	In a new string, saves a structured version of the arguments
format_to	Through an output iterator, it generates a formatted representation of its parameters
format_to_n	An output iterator generates a formatted representation of its parameters that do not exceed the size limit
formatted_size	specifies how many characters are required to hold the formatted representation of the parameters

Extensibility support and implementation detail:

vformat	Type-erased argument representation in a non-template version of std::format
vformat_to	std::format to non-template version with type-erased argument representation
basic_format_arg	a class template that gives user-defined formatters access to a formatting parameter
formatter	Formatting rules for a certain type are defined by a class template

(Continued)

basic_format_ parse_ contextformat_ parse_ contextwformat_ parse_context	condition of string parser formatting
basic_format_ contextformat_ contextwformat_ context	All formatting parameters and the output iterator are included in the formatting state
visit_format_arg	For user-defined formatters, an argument visitation interface is provided
make_format_ argsmake_ wformat_args	Converts to format args a type-erased object referencing all formatting parameters
basic_format_ argsformat_ argswformat_args	All formatting arguments are accessible through this class
format_error	Formatting problems cause an exception of this type to be thrown

Text remains one of the most common ways for people to interact with computer systems, despite the growth of graphical and voice user interfaces, and programming languages give a range of methods for text formatting. When learning a new programming language, we frequently begin by building a "Hello, World!" program that produces simple formatted output.

The printf family of methods inherited from C and the I/O streams library is both standard APIs for doing formatted output in C++ (iostreams). While iostreams are typically the preferred way of creating formatted output in C++ due to their safety and flexibility, printf offers certain benefits, such as a more natural function call API, separation of formatted message and parameters, and frequently less source and binary code.

Example:

```
string message = fmt::format("Answer
is {}.", 32);
```

STRING SYNTAX FOR DESIGN FORMAT

The printf format string syntax is perhaps the most widely used among computer languages, and printf is inherited from C++. The printf syntax has the advantage of being well-known among programmers. However, it has a number of flaws in its current state:

- Many format specifiers, such as hh, h, l, j, and others, are solely used to communicate type information. They are unnecessary in type-safe formatting and would make specification and parsing excessively difficult.

- For user-defined types, there is no standard mechanism to expand the syntax.

- There are minor differences between various implementations. Some systems, for example, do not accept POSIX positional parameters.

- It's impossible to use "percent" in a custom format specifier, such as for put time-like time formatting.

While it is feasible to fix these concerns while retaining a close similarity to the original printf format, this would break compatibility and maybe more confusing to users than creating a new syntax.

Some of the Benefits Include

- Mini-language that is consistent and easy to understand, with a concentration on formatting rather than type information.

- Extensibility of user-defined types and support for custom format string parameters from a location.

- Both locale-specific and locale-independent formats are supported.

- Formatting improvements include better alignment control, fill character and binary format.

The syntax is expressive enough to allow for automatic translation of most printf format strings. The following table shows the relationship between printf and the new syntax.

printf	new	
−	<	
+	+	
space	space	
#	#	
0	0	
hh	unused	
h	unused	
l	unused	
ll	unused	
j	unused	(Continued)

printf	new
z	unused
t	unused
L	unused
c	c (optional)
s	s (optional)
d	d (optional)
i	d (optional)
o	o
x	x
X	X
u	d (optional)
f	f
F	F
e	e
E	E
a	a
A	A
g	g (optional)
G	G
n	unused
p	p (optional)

In printf and the suggested syntax, width and precision are expressed similarly, with the exception that the run-time value is provided by * in the former and in the latter, potentially with the index of the argument inside the brackets.

Most of the specifiers are the same, making the transition from printf much easier. The alignment specification is a notable distinction. The suggested syntax provides for the left, center, and right alignment using the characters ", ", and '>', which is more expressive than the printf syntax.

The latter only allows for left and right alignment (the default).

The example below utilizes center alignment and the character '*' as a fill character:

"**********centered**********" is the output of fmt::format(":*30", "centered"); With printf, the same formatting is difficult to obtain.

EXTENSIBILITY

The API and the format string syntax are both designed to be extensible. Users can add parsing and formatting techniques for these types, and the mini-language can be expanded to include user-defined types.

A replacement field in a format string has the following general syntax:

```
replacement-field ::= '{' [arg-id] [':'
format-spec] '}'
```

For built-in types, format-spec is preset; however, for user-defined types, it can be modified.

By adding a format value overload for tm:

```
void format_value(fmt::buffer& buf, const
tm& tm, fmt::context& ctx);
```

The format value function parses the section of the format string that corresponds to the current argument and uses the format to or the buffer API to format the value into buf.

If the ostream << insertion operator is available, the default implementation of format value uses it.

SAFETY

Instead of using the cstdarg> method, formatting functions use variadic templates. The type information is automatically collected and given to formatters, ensuring type
safety and eliminating the need for many printf specifiers.
To avoid the typical printf buffer overflow problems, buffer
management is automated.

LOCALE SUPPORT

Many use cases do not necessitate internationalization
but do necessitate fast throughput when delivered via
a server, as mentioned in P0067R1: Elementary string
conversions. Various text-based interchange formats are
among them, such as JSON or XML. N4412: iostreams
Shortcomings underlines the importance of locale-independent techniques for converting integers to strings
and floating-point values to strings. As a result, a user
should have easy discretion over employing locales during formatting.

POSITIONAL ARGUMENTS

Because various languages have varied word orders, the
ability to alter formatting arguments is crucial for localiza-
tion. Consider the following scenario:

```
printf("String '%s' has %d characters\n",
string, length(string)));
```

POSIX positional parameters are used. These positioning
specifiers, however, are not transferable. Because they

are interleaved with sections of the literal text, C++ I/O streams do not enable such reordering of parameters by design:

```
cout << "String '" << string << "' has "
<< length(string) << " characters\n";
```

Positional and automatically numbered arguments are both allowed in the present proposal, Example:

```
fmt::format("String '{}' has {}
characters\n", string, length(string)));
```

PERFORMANCE

The performance of the formatting library was taken into consideration when it was created. It aims to keep the number of virtual function calls and dynamic memory allocations per formatting operation as low as possible. It should be feasible to eliminate them entirely by using an appropriate API if formatting output can fit within a fixed-size buffer created on the stack.

To this purpose, the fmt::basic buffer template is used to represent a buffer abstraction. A buffer is a continuous piece of memory that may be accessed directly and can increase in size if necessary. During formatting, just one virtual function, grow, has to be called, and it's only when the buffer isn't big enough.

Locale-independent formatting is also more efficient to implement than locale-aware formatting. However, rather than improving performance, the former's primary objective is to serve certain use cases.

BINARY FOOTPRINT

Each formatting function that utilizes variadic templates is a tiny inline wrapper over its non-variadic equivalent to reducing binary code size. This wrapper uses fmt::make args to construct an object representing an array of argument references, then calls the non-variadic function to perform the real job. The format variadic function, for example, uses the vformat variable.

If the number of arguments is minimal, several argument-type codes can be merged and given as a single integer to a formatting function. Because the kinds of arguments are known at build time, this can be an integer constant for which no code is written except to store it according to calling conventions.

This will produce a compact per-call binary code that sets argument pointers and packed argument type codes on the stack and executes a formatting function, assuming a decent optimizing compiler.

NULL-TERMINATED STRING VIEW

Instead of using a basic string view, the formatting library utilizes a basic cstring view, which is a null-terminated string view. The code is somewhat smaller and faster because the string size, which isn't utilized, doesn't have to be computed and provided. It's also easier to parse with a termination character.

Header <format> synopsis

```
namespace std {
namespace fmt {
```

```
template <class Cont>
class basic_arg;

template <class Visit, class Cont>
see below vis(Visi&& vis, basic_
arg<Cont> arg);

template <class Cont, class ...Args>
class arg_store;

template <class Cont>
class basic_args;

template <class Char>
class basic_cont;

typedef basic_context<char> context;
typedef basic_args<cont> args;

template <class ...Args>
arg_store<context, Args...> make_
args(const Args&... args);

template <class Cont, class ...Args>
arg_store<Context, Args...> make_
args(const Args&... args);

template <class Char>
class basic_buffer;

typedef basic_buffer<char> buffer;

template <class Char>
class basic_cstring_view;

typedef basic_cstring_view<char>
cstring_view;
```

```
class format_error;

template <class ...Args>
string format(cstring_view format_str,
const Args&... args);

string vformat(cstring_view format_str,
args args);

template <class ...Args>
string format_to(buffer& buf, cstring_
view format_str, const Args&... args);

string vformat_to(buffer& buf, cstring_
view format_str, args args);

template <class Char, class T>
void format_value(basic_buffer<Char>&
buf, const T& value, basic_
context<Char>& ctx);
}   // namespace fmt
}   // namespace std
```

FORMAT STRING SYNTAX

Replacement fields are included in curly brackets in format strings. Anything not included in brackets is considered literal text, and it is copied to the output unmodified. By doubling: {{ and }} and, a brace character can be incorporated in the actual text.

A replacement field's syntax:

```
replacement-field is '{' [arg-id] [':'
format-spec] '}'
```

```
arg-id  is integer
integer  is digit+
digit is '0'...'9'
```

The replacement field can begin with an arg-id, which identifies the argument whose value is to be prepared and included in the output rather than the replacement field. Optionally, a format-spec is appended to the arg-id, which is preceded by a colon ":". These define a format for the replacement value that is not the default.

Here are some examples of basic format strings:

```
"First, thou shalt count to {0}"
"Bring me a {}"
"From {} to {}"
```

The format-spec parameter determines the presentation of the value, including field width, alignment, padding, decimal precision, and other features. Each value type can specify its own formatting mini-language or format-spec interpretation.

FORMAT SPECIFICATION MINI-LANGUAGE

Format specifications are used to describe how individual values are displayed in replacement fields within a format string. Every formattable type can specify how the format specification should be interpreted.

Although some of the formatting choices are only available by numeric types, most built-in types implement the following options for format requirements.

A standard format specifier takes the following general form:

```
format-spec ::=   [[fill] align] [sign]
["#"] ["0"] [width] ["." precision] [type]
fill         ::=  <a character other than
"{' or '}">
align        ::=  "<",   ">",   "=",   "^"
sign         ::=  "+",   "-",   " "
width        ::=  integer,  "{' arg-id '}"
precision    ::=  integer,  "{' arg-id '}"
type         ::=  int-type,  "a" "A",  "c",
"e",  "E",  "f",  "F",  "g",  "G",  "p",
"s"
int-type     ::=  "b",  "B",  "d",  "o",
"x",  "X"
```

Any character other than '{' or '}' can be used as the fill character. The character after the fill character, which must be one of the alignment possibilities, indicates a fill character. The fill character and the alignment option are presumed to be missing if the second character of format-spec is not a valid alignment option.

The following are the definitions of the various alignment options:

Option	Meaning
"<"	Within the remaining space, forces the field to be left-aligned.
">"	Within the available space, forces the field to be right-aligned.

"="	The padding is forced to come after the sign but before the numerals. This is used to print fields with the +000000120 format. Only numeric types can use this alignment option.
"^"	The field is forced to be centered in the given area.

Unless a minimum field width is specified, the field width will always be the same as the data used to fill it; therefore, the alignment option is irrelevant in this case.

Only number types have the sign option, which might be one of the following:

Option	Meaning
"+"	This indicates that a sign should be used for both positive as well as negative numbers.
"-"	This indicates that a sign should be used only for negative numbers (this is the default behavior).
space	This indicates that a leading space should be used on positive numbers and a minus sign on negative numbers.

The "#" option forces the converter to use the other form. For each kind, the alternative form is specified differently. This option supports only integer and floating-point types. This option adds the prefix "0b" ("0B"), "0", or "0x" ("0X") to the output value for integers and to binary, octal, or hexadecimal output. The case of the type specifier determines whether the prefix is lower-case or upper-case; the prefix "0x" is used for the type "x", whereas "0X" is used for the type "X". The alternate form always causes the conversion output to contain a decimal-point character, even if no digits follow it, for floating-point values.

In most cases, a decimal-point character only appears in the output of these conversions if a digit follows it. Furthermore, trailing zeros are not eliminated from the result for "g" and "G" conversions.

The decimal integer width defines the minimum field width. If no field width is given, the content will decide the field width.

Sign-aware zero-padding for numeric types is enabled by preceding the width field with a zero ("0") character. This is the same as using the fill character "0" with the alignment type "=".

For a floating-point value formatted with "f" or "F", the precision is a decimal number that indicates how many digits should be displayed after the decimal point. A floating-point number is formatted with "g" or "G" before and after the decimal point. The field determines the maximum field size for non-number kinds, or how many characters will be used from the field content. Integer, character, Boolean, and pointer values are not permitted to be precise.

Finally, the type affects how the information is displayed. The following string presentation types are available:

Type	Meaning
"s"	This is a string format. This is the default string type, and it can be omitted.
none	The same as "s".

The following character display types are available:

Type	Meaning
"c"	Format for characters. This is the default character type, and it can be removed.
none	The same as "c".

The following are the integer presentation kinds that are available:

Type	Meaning
"b"	Binary is a kind of data. This function returns an integer in base 2. The prefix "0b" is added to the output value when the "#" option is used with this type.
"B"	Binary is a kind of data. This function returns an integer in base 2. The prefix "0B" is added to the output value when the "#" option is used with this type.
"d"	Integer in decimal form. Returns a number in base ten.
"o"	The format is octal. The number in base 8 is returned.
"x"	The hexadecimal system is used. The number is written in base 16, with the digits above nine written in lower case letters. The prefix "0x" is added to the output value when the "#" option is used with this type.
"X"	The hexadecimal system is used. The number is shown in base 16, with the digits above nine represented by upper-case letters. The prefix

	"0X" is added to the output value when the "#" option is used with this type.
"n"	Number. This is the same as "d", except instead of inserting the necessary amount of separator characters, it utilizes the buffer's locale.
none	The same as "d".

Character and Boolean values can also be utilized with integer presentation types. If the presentation type is not provided, Boolean values are presented using textual representation, either true or false.

For floating-point values, the following presentation formats are available:

Type	Meaning
"a"	Format for floating-point numbers in hexadecimal. For numbers more than nine, prints the number in base 16 with the prefix "0x" and lower-case letters. The exponent is indicated by the letter "p".
"A"	It's the same as "a", but with upper-case letters for the prefix, numbers above nine, and an exponent indication.
"e"	Notation with exponents. The number is printed in scientific notation, with the letter "e" indicating the exponent.
"E"	Notation with exponents. It's the same as "e", only the separator character is an upper-case "E".
"f"	This is a fixed point. The number is shown as a fixed-point number.

"F"	This is a fixed point. Converts nan to NAN and inf to INF, much like "f".
"g"	This is a general format. This method rounds the number to p significant digits and then displays the result in fixed-point or scientific notation, depending on the magnitude, with a precision of p >= 1. A precision of zero is considered to be the same as a precision of one.
"n"	Number. This is similar to "g", except it utilizes the buffer's locale to insert the proper amount of separator characters.
none	The same as "g".

The following are the many sorts of pointer presentations that are available:

Type	Meaning
"p"	Format for a pointer. This is the default pointer type, and it can be omitted.
none	The same as "p".

FORMATTING FUNCTIONS

- template <class ...Args>

  ```
  string format(cstring_view format_str,
  const Args&... args);
  ```

- **Effects:** The method returns a string object created from the format string parameter format str, with each replacement field replaced with the character representation of the argument it refers to, formatted according to the field's specification.

- **Returned:** The formatted string is returned.

- **Thrown:** If format str is not a valid format string, format error is thrown.

    - string vformat(cstring_view format_str, fmt::args args);

- **Effects:** The method returns a string object created from the format string parameter format str. Each replacement field is replaced with the character representation of the argument it refers to, formatted according to the field specification.

- **Returned:** The formatted string is returned by this method.

- **Thrown:** If format str isn't a valid format string, format error will be thrown.

FORMATTING ARGUMENT

```
template <class Context>
class basic_arg {
public:
  basic_arg();

  explicit operator bool() const noexcept;

  bool is_integral() const;
  bool is_numeric() const;
  bool is_pointer() const;
};
```

An object of type basic argContext> represents a formatting argument parameterized on a formatting context. It can store one of the following sorts of values:

```
int
unsigned int
integral types larger than int
bool
Char
double
floating-point types larger than double
const char*
string_view
basic_string_view<Char>
const void*
```

where Char denotes the typename Context::char type. The value may be obtained using the next section's visiting interface.

- basic_arg();

    Effects: Creates a basic_arg object that isn't a reference to an argument.

    Postcondition: !(*this).

    ```
    explicit operator bool() const
    noexcept;
    ```

    Returns: If *this relates to an argument, it is true; otherwise, it is false.

- bool is_integral() const;

  Returns: True if *this represents an integral type argument.

- bool is_numeric() const;

  Returns: If *this represents a numeric type argument, then true.

- bool is_pointer() const;

  Returns: If *this represents an argument of type const void*, then it is true.

- **Complexity:** The number of potential value types for a formatting parameter has no bearing on the invocation of is_integral, is_numeric, and is_pointer.

FORMATTING ARGUMENT VISITATION

- template <class Visit, class Cont>

  ```
  see below vis(Visit&& vis, basic_
  arg<Cont> arg);
  ```

- **Requires:** For all possible value types of a formatting parameter, the expression in the effects section must be a valid expression of the same type otherwise the program is ill-formed.

- **Effects:** Allow value to be the formatting parameter arg's value. INVOKE(forward(vis), value); returns the result.

- **Remarks:** The return type is the type that all INVOKE expressions in the Effects section have in common. Visitors should utilize type characteristics to manage various kinds since precise value types are implementation-defined.

- **Complexity:** The number of potential values types of a formatting argument has no impact on the callable object's invocation.

Example:

```
auto uint_value = visit([](auto value) {
  if constexpr
(is_unsigned_v<delctype(value)>)
    return value;
  return 0;
}, arg);
```

CLASS TEMPLATE arg_store

- template <class Context, class ...Args>

```
class arg_store;
```

Formatting parameters or references to them are stored in an object of type arg_store.

CLASS TEMPLATE basic_args

- template <class Context>

```
class basic_args {
public:
  typedef implementation-defined
size_type;
```

```
basic_args() noexcept;

template <class ...Args>
basic_args(const arg_store<Context,
Args...>& store);

basic_arg<Context> operator[](size_
type i) const;
};
```

Access to formatting parameters is provided via an object of type basic_args. The parameters are not copied when a basic_args object is copied.

- basic_args() noexcept;

  Effects: Constructs an empty basic_args object.

  Postcondition: !(*this)[0].

- template <class ...Args>

  ```
  basic_args(const arg_store<Context,
  Args...>& store);
  ```

  Effects: Constructs a basic_args object that gives you access to the store's arguments.

- basic_arg<Context> operator[](size_type i) const;

  Requires: i <= the basic_args object's representation of the number of formatting parameters.

  Returns: If I is the number of arguments, a basic_arg object represents an argument at index i. Otherwise, an empty basic_arg object is returned.

FUNCTION TEMPLATE make_args

- template <class ...Args>

```
arg_store<context, Args...> make_
args(const Args&... args);
```

Effects: The method returns an arg_store object that contains pointers to or copies of args formatting parameters.

Returns: The formatting parameters are used to create the arg_store object.

FORMATTING CONTEXT

- template <class Char>

```
class basic_context {
public:
  typedef Char char_type;
  typedef basic_args<basic_context>
args_type;

  basic_context(const Char* format_str,
args_type args);

  const Char*& ptr();

  args_type args() const;
};
```

Basic_context is a user-defined type formatting context that provides access to formatting parameters as well as the current position in the parsed format string.

- basic_context(const Char* format_str, args_type args);
    Constructs a basic context object that contains pointers to the formatting arguments and the format string.

    Postcondition: ptr() == format_str.

- const Char*& ptr();
    The current location in the format string being parsed is returned as a pointer.

- args_type args() const;
    Returns a copy of the args object provided to the basic_context function Object.

FORMATTING BUFFER

- template <class Char>

```
class basic_buffer {
public:
  typedef implementation-defined
size_type;

  virtual ~basic_buffer();

  size_type size() const noexcept;
  size_type capacity() const noexcept;

  void resize(size_type sz);
  void reserve(size_type n);

  Char* data() noexcept;
  const Char* data() const noexcept;

  void push_back(const Char& x);
```

```
template <class InputIterator>
void append(InputIterator first,
InputIterator last);
virtual locale locale() const;

protected:
basic_buffer() noexcept;

void set(Char* s, size_type n)
noexcept;

virtual void grow(size_type n) = 0;
};
```

FORMAT STRING

- template <class Char>

```
class basic_cstring_view {
public:
  basic_cstring_view(const basic_
string<Char>& str);
  basic_cstring_view(const Char* str);

  const Char* c_str() const noexcept;
};
```

USER-DEFINED TYPES

If a format string refers to a user-defined type object, as in:

```
X x;
string s = format("{}", x);
```

buf, x, ctx where buf is a reference to the formatting buffer, x is a const reference, and ctx is a reference to the formatting context. In the parsed format string, ptr() will point to one of the following positions:

- ':' preceding format-spec for the current argument

- '}' if no format-spec is present.

The format value function should read format-spec, format the argument, and advance ctx. ptr() to ", which terminates the current argument's replacement field.

ERROR REPORTING

```
class format_error : public runtime_error
{
public:
  explicit format_error(const string&
what_arg);
  explicit format_error(const char*
what_arg);
};
```

The class format_error specifies the kind of objects thrown as exceptions when the formatting library encounters an error.

In this chapter, we have learned how to convert data between numeric and string types, the limits and other properties of numeric types, and how to create cooked and raw user-defined literals. We also learnt how to develop a library of string helpers and what std::format is for formatting text.

CHAPTER 4

Exploring C++ Functions

IN THIS CHAPTER

➤ Defaulted and Deleted Functions

➤ Lambdas and Standard Algorithms

➤ Writing a Function Template with a Variable of Number of Arguments

➤ Using Fold Expressions to Simplify Variadic Function Templates

➤ Implementing the Higher-order Functions Map and Fold

In the previous chapter, we learned how to convert data between numeric and string types, the limits and other

DOI: 10.1201/9781003214762-4

properties of numeric types, and how to create cooked and raw user-defined literals in this chapter. We also learn how to develop a library of string helpers and what std::format is for formatting text.

In this chapter, we will turn our attention to topics such as C++ functions, including function handling, expressions, and more.

WHAT IS THE DEFINITION OF A DEFAULTED FUNCTION?

Explicitly defaulted function declaration is a new kind of function declaration introduced in the C++11 standard that allows you to define a function as expressly defaulted in appending the "=default"; specifier to the end of the function declaration. This causes the compiler to create default implementations for expressly defaulted functions, which are more efficient than human implementations. When we define a parameterized function Object, the compiler does not build a default function Object. In this instance, we may construct a default one by using the default specifier. The code below illustrates how to:

Example:

```
#include <iostream>
using namespace std;

class B {
public:
    // A user-defined
    // parameterized constructor
    B(int y)
    {
```

```
        cout << " Parameterized
constructor";
    }

    // Using the default specifier to
instruct
    B() = default;
};

int main()
{
    // executes using defaulted
constructor
    B b;
    // uses parameterized constructor
    B y(1);
    return 0;
}
```

Output:

```
Parameterized constructor
```

We didn't have to provide the body of the function Object B() in the previous example since the compiler created a default implementation of the function by attaching the specifier "=default".

WHAT ARE THE LIMITATIONS OF MAKING FUNCTIONS DEFAULT?

A defaulted function must be a special member function (default function Object, destructor, and so on), or it must not have any default parameters. Non-special member functions, for example, cannot be defaulted, as seen in the following code:

Example:

```
class B {
public:

    // func is not a special member,
Error
    int func() = default;

    // constructor B(int, int) is not
    // a special member, Error
    B(int, int) = default;

    // Error, constructor, has a
default argument.
    B(int = 0) = default;
};
int main()
{
    return 0;
}
```

What are the benefits of using "=default" when we could use "{}" to leave the function body empty?

Even though the two may act similarly, there are still advantages to utilizing default versus leaving the constructor's body empty. The following points will show you how:

- Even if it does nothing, adding a user-defined function Object to a type makes it neither an aggregate nor trivial. You must use "= default" if you wish your class to be an aggregate or trivial type (or, through transitivity, a POD type).

- It's also possible to use "= default" with copy constructors and destructors. For example, an empty copy function will not perform the same as a defaulting copy function (which will perform a memberwise copy of its members). It is simpler to comprehend code if the "= default" syntax is used consistently for these special member functions.

DELETED FUNCTION

Before C++ 11, the delete operator had just one purpose: to deallocate dynamically allocated memory.

Another usage of this operator was introduced in the C++ 11 standard: To stop a member function from being used. The =delete; specifier is appended to the end of the function definition to accomplish this.

An expressly deleted function is a member function whose usage has been disallowed by using the "=delete" specifier.

This is generally done to implicit functions, though it is not restricted to them. The following are some instances of tasks where this functionality is proper:

- **Disabling copy constructors**

    Example:
    ```
    #include <iostream>
    using namespace std;

    class B {
    public:
    ```

```
    B(int y): m(y)
    {
    }

    // Delete the copy constructor
    B(const B&) = delete;

    // Delete the copy assignment
operator
    B& operator=(const B&) = delete;
    int n;
};

int main()
{
    B a1(1), b2(2), b3(3);

    // Error, the usage of the copy
    // assignment operator is disabled
    b1 = b2;

    // Error, the usage of the
    // copy constructor is disabled
    b3 = B(b2);
    return 0;
}
```

- **Disabling undesirable argument conversion**

Example:

```
// delete operator using type
conversion
#include <iostream>
using namespace std;
```

```cpp
class B {
public:
    B(int) {}

    // deleted function.
    // B(double) isn't defined,
    // the B(int) accept any double
value
    // convert it to an int
    B(double) = delete;
};

int main()
{
    B B1(1);

    // Error, conversion from
    // double to class A is disabled.
    B B2(100.1);
    return 0;
}
```

It's crucial to remember that a removed function is still inline. A function's erased definition must be the function's initial declaration. To put it another way, designating a function as removed should be done as follows:

```cpp
class D
{
public:
        D(D& d) = delete;
};
```

Attempting to define a function removed in the following manner will result in an error:

Example:

```
// function as deleted
class D
{
public:
    D();
};

// Error, the deleted definition
// of function C must be the first
// declaration of the function.
D::D() = delete;
```

WHAT ARE THE BENEFITS OF REMOVING FUNCTIONS EXPLICITLY?

Delete special member functions to make it easier to prevent the compiler from creating special member functions we don't want. (As seen in the example "Disabling copy constructors").

Problematic type promotions are prevented from calling an undesired function by deleting regular member or non-member functions (as illustrated in the "Disabling undesirable argument conversion" example).

WHAT IS LAMBDAS?

It's a simple method to create a functor or anonymous function object. It's useful since we can define it locally and call it or provide it as a parameter to a function.

Lambda is also simple to read because everything is in one location.

Expressions Using a Lambda

In C++, a lambda is defined as follows:

Example:

```cpp
auto plus_one = [](const int value)
{
    return value + 1;
};

assert(plus_one(2) == 3);
```

Under the hood, plus one is a functor in this code.

Functor or Function Object

A functor, often known as a function object, is a construct that allows an object to be called as if it were a regular function.

"Ordinary function" is the crucial phrase here. To implement a functor in C++, we can overload the operation (). Here's a functor that works similarly to our lambda:

Example:

```cpp
struct Oneplus
{
    int op()(const int value) const
    {
        return val + 1;
    }
};
```

```cpp
int main ()
{
    Oneplus Oneplus;
    assert(Oneplus(2) == 3);

    return 0;
}
```

One of the benefits of utilizing a functor over a regular function is to access the object's internal member variables and functions.

It will be obvious when we wish to write functions like "plus one", "plus two", and so on. We don't have to specify numerous functions with different names when we use a functor.

Example:

```cpp
class P
{
public:
    P(const int data) :
        data(data) {}

    int op() (const int value) const
    {
        return val + data;
    }
private:
    const int d;
};

int main ()
{
```

```
P onePlus(1);
assert(Oneplus (2) == 3);

P twoPlus(2);
assert(twoPlus(2) == 4);

return 0;
}
```

As you can see, it seems to be a call to a standard function from the caller's perspective.

What does it seem like from the machine's perspective? Because a functor is an object, it contains variables and functions for its members. The basic operation is as follows:

```
int one_plus(const int val)
{
  return val + 1;
}
```

Lambdas vs. Functors

Why do we need lambdas if we already have a functor that is sometimes better than a regular function?

Lambda makes it easier to write a functor. It's syntactic sugar for a functor with no name. It lowers the amount of boilerplate code that must be written in a functor.

Example:

```
auto p = [data=1](const int val)
    {
        return val + data;
    };

assert(p(2) == 3);
```

From our functor above, we can eliminate a lot of boiler-plate code. Our functor has the following appearance:

```
int OnePlus::op()(const OnePlus* this,
const int val)
{
  return val + this->data;
}
```

So, how's it doing with our lambda? This is what it looks like if we define our lambda within our primary function:

```
int mainfun::lambda::op()(const lambda*
hidden, const int val)
{
  return val + hidden->data;
}
```

Except for the name, it's quite identical to our functor. However, now we understand that our lambda is nothing more than a reduced version of a functor with no name.

Another thing to note is that the concealed pointer's name isn't this since this keyword is reserved for the object in the outer scope.

THE FUNCTION OF A CALLBACK

Callback functions are frequently written using both functors and lambdas. They come in handy when working with Standard Template Library (STL) algorithms, when we wish to convert data contained in a std::vector, for example.

Example:

```cpp
class P
{
public:
    Plus(const int data) :
        data(data) {}

    int op()(const int val) const
    {
        return val + data;
    }
private:
    const int data;
};

int mainfun ()
{
    Plus one_plus(1);
    std::vector<int> test_data = {4, 2,
3, 1};

    std::transform(test_data.begin(),
test_data.end(), test_data.begin(),
one_plus);
    return 0;
}
```

To create/initialize member variables, capture variables:

We should consider a lambda as an object and utilize the capture "[]" approach to construct and initialize member variables. We may just write a variable in "[]" to create and initialize it:

Example:

```
auto return_one = [value=1](){ return
value; };
```

PASSING LAMBDAS AS ARGUMENTS

We've already seen how to pass a lambda as an argument by converting it to a raw function pointer. However, this only works for lambdas that aren't captured.

Lambdas can be sent as parameters to functions in two ways:

- The STL method, using a template

- Use the std::function

The STL Method, Using a Template

Example:

```
template<typename D>
int Plus(const int b, D fp)
{
    return fp(a);
}

int main ()
{
    auto one_plus = [value=1](const
int y) -> int
    {
        return y + val;
    };
```

```
int res = Plus(3, one_plus);
assert(res==5);

return 0;
}
```

Use the std::function

Example:

```
int Plusone(const int a,
std::function<int(const int)> fp)
{
    return fp(a);
}

int main ()
{
    auto one_plus = [value=1](const
int y) -> int
    {
        return y + value;
    };

    int res = Plusone(4, one_plus);
    assert(res==5);

    return 0;
}
```

STANDARD TEMPLATE LIBRARY ALGORITHM

Only knowing about STL containers is of little help to individuals who desire to excel in competitive programming unless they know all STL has to offer.

For any < algorithm > library functions, STL provides an ocean of algorithms: Please see this page for further information.

The following are some of the most often used vector algorithms, as well as some of the most helpful in Competitive Programming:

Algorithms that do not manipulate data:

- To sort the provided vector, use sort(first iterator, last iterator).

- To reverse a vector, use reverse(first iterator, last iterator).

- ***max element (first iterator, last iterator):** Returns the vector's maximum element.

- ***min element (first iterator, last iterator):** Returns the vector's minimal element.

- **accumulate(first iterator, last iterator, sum start value):** Performs vector element summing.

Example:

```
#include <algorithm>
#include <iostream>
#include <vector>
#include <numeric>
using namespace std;

int main()
{
    // Initializing array values
    int arra[] = {20, 30, 15, 32,
54, 25};
```

```cpp
    int num= sizeof(arr)/
sizeof(arr[0]);
    vector<int> vect(arra, arra+n);

    cout << "Vector: ";
    for (int i=0; i<num; i++)
        cout << vect[i] << " ";

    // Sorting in Ascending order
    sort(vect.begin(), vect.end());

    cout << "\nVector after sorting
is: ";
    for (int i=0; i<num; i++)
    cout << vect[i] << " ";

    // Reversing
    reverse(vect.begin(), vect.
end());

    cout << "\nVector after reversing
is: ";
    for (int i=0; i<6; i++)
        cout << vect[i] << " ";

    cout << "\nMaximum element: ";
    cout << *max_element(vect.
begin(), vect.end());

    cout << "\nMinimum element: ";
    cout << *min_element(vect.
begin(), vect.end());

    return 0;
}
```

Output:

```
Vector is: 50, 40, 30, 20, 10, 5
Vector after sorting is: 5 10 20 30
40 50
Vector after reversing is: 50 40 230
15 10 5
Maximum element of vector is: 50
Minimum element of vector is: 5
```

- **count(first iterator, last iterator, x):** Counts the number of times x appears in the vector.

- **find(first iterator, last iterator, x):** Returns an iterator to the first occurrence of x in the vector and pointers to the vector's last address (name of vector),end()) if the element isn't in the vector.

Example:

```cpp
#include <algorithm>
#include <iostream>
#include <vector>
using namespace std;

int mainfun()
{
    // array values
    int arra[] = {30, 20, 5, 32, 24,
72, 51};
    int num = sizeof(arra)/
sizeof(arra[0]);
    vector<int> vect(arra, arra+num);
```

```
    cout << "Occurrences of 32 in
vector : ";

    cout << count(vect.begin(), vect.
end(), 20);

    // find() returns iterator to
last address
    find(vect.begin(), vect.end(),5)
!= vect.end()?
                        cout << "\n
found":
                        cout << "\n not
found";

    return 0;
}
```

Output:

```
Occurrences of 32 in vector: 4
```

- **binary search(first iterator, last iterator, x):** Determines if x is present in the sorted vector.

- **lower bound(first iterator, last iterator, x):** returns an iterator pointing to the first element in the range [first,last] with a value greater than or equal to x.

- **upper bound(first iterator, last iterator, x):** produces an iterator pointing to the first element with a value larger than "x" in the range [first,last].

Example:

```cpp
#include <algorithm>
#include <iostream>
#include <vector>
using namespace std;

int main()
{
    // Initializing array values
    int arra[] = {30, 20, 5, 32, 24,
72, 42, 45};
    int num = sizeof(arr)/
sizeof(arra[0]);
    vector<int> vect(arra, arra+num);

    // Sort the array
    sort(vect.begin(), vect.end());

    // Returns the first occurrence
    auto q = lower_bound(vect.
begin(), vect.end(), 20);

    auto p = upper_bound(vect.
begin(), vect.end(), 20);

    cout << "The lower bound is at
position: ";
    cout << q-vect.begin() << endl;

    cout << "The upper bound is at
position: ";
    cout << p-vect.begin() << endl;

    return 0;
}
```

Output:

```
The lower bound is at position: 1
The upper bound is at position: 2
```

ALGORITHMS FOR MANIPULATION

- **arr.erase(position to be removed):** Removes a chosen element from a vector and resizes and adjusts the vector elements appropriately.

- **arr.erase(unique(arr.begin(),arr.end()),arr.end()):** This deletes duplicate occurrences on a single line in a sorted vector.

Example:

```cpp
#include <algorithm>
#include <iostream>
#include <vector>
using namespace std;

int main()
{
    // Initializing vector with array values
    int arra[] = {30, 20, 5, 32, 24, 72, 42, 45};
    int num = sizeof(arra)/ sizeof(arra[0]);
    vector<int> vect(arra, arra+num);

    cout << "The vector is :";
    for (int c=0; c<6; c++)
        cout << vect[c]<<" ";
```

```
    // Delete second element of
vector
    vect.erase(vect.begin()+1);

    cout << "\nVector after erasing
element: ";
    for (int c=0; c<vect.size();
c++)
        cout << vect[c] << " ";

    // sorting to enable use of
unique()
    sort(vect.begin(), vect.end());

    cout << "\nVector before removing
duplicate "
            " occurrences: ";
    for (int c=0; c<vect.size();
c++)
        cout << vect[i] << " ";

    // Deletes the duplicate
occurrences
    vect.erase(unique(vect.
begin(),vect.end()),vect.end());

    cout << "\nVector after deleting
duplicates: ";
    for (int c=0; c< vect.size();
c++)
        cout << vect[c] << " ";

    return 0;
}
```

Output:

```
The vector is: 30 20 5 32 24 72
Vector after erasing element: 30 5
32 24 72 42 45
Vector before removing duplicate
occurrences: 5 24 30 32 42 45 72
Vector after deleting duplicates: 5
24 30 32 42 45 72
```

- **next permutation(first iterator, last iterator):** This function changed the vector's permutation to the next one.

- **prev permutation(first iterator, last iterator):** This changed the vector's permutation to the previous one.

- **distance(first_iterator, desired_position):** Returns the distance between the first iterator and the desired position. This method is quite handy when looking for an index.

Example:

```cpp
#include <algorithm>
#include <iostream>
#include <vector>
using namespace std;

int main()
{
    // Initializing array values
    int arra[] = {30, 20, 5, 32, 24,
72, 42, 45};
```

```
    int num = sizeof(arra)/
sizeof(arra[0]);
    vector<int> vect(arra, arra+num);

    // Return distance of first to
maximum element
    cout << "Distance between first
to max element: ";
    cout << distance(vect.begin(),
                    max_element(vect.
begin(), vect.end())));
    return 0;
}
```

Output:

```
Distance between first to max
element: 5
```

VARIADIC FUNCTION

Variadic functions take a variable number of arguments, for example, std::printf.

An ellipsis comes after the list of parameters, e.g. int printf(const char* format...);, which may be preceded by an optional comma, to declare a variadic function. For more information on the syntax, automated argument conversions, and alternatives, see Variadic arguments.

The following library facilities are given to access the variadic arguments from the function body:

va_start	Access to variadic function arguments is enabled
va_arg	accesses the next argument of a variadic function
va_copy	duplicates the variadic function parameters
(C++11)	

(Continued)

| **va_end** | The traversal of the variadic function parameters comes to a conclusion |
| **va_list** | contains the data that va_start, va_arg, va_end, and va_copy (typedef) require |

Syntax:

```
temp(typename arg, typename... args)
return_type func_name(arg variable1,
args... variable2)
```

Example:

```cpp
#include <iostream>
using namespace std;

// To handle recursive Variadic
function Template
void print()
{
    cout << "Empty function and "
            "called at last\n" ;
}

// Variadic function takes variable
number of arguments and prints
template <typename T, typename...
Types>
void print(T var1, Types... var2)
{
    cout << var1 << endl ;

    print(var2...) ;
}
```

```
// Driver code
int main()
{
    print(2, 3, 4.14, "Pass any "
            "number of arguments");

    return 0;
}
```

Output:

```
2
3
4.14
Pass any number of arguments
Empty function and called at last
```

EXPRESSIONS

This section covers C++ expressions, which are collections of operators and operands that serve one or more of the following purposes:

The operands are used to calculate a value.

Objects or functions are designated.

Creating "unintended consequences" (Side effects are any activities other than evaluating the expression, such as changing an object's value.)

Operators in C++ can be overloaded, and their semantics can be customized. Their order of precedence and the number of operands they accept, however, cannot be changed. Without becoming overloaded, this section discusses the syntax and semantics of operators as supplied by the language.

Expressions of Many Kinds

The following are the different types of C++ expressions

- **Expressions that are fundamental:** These are the essential elements upon which all other expressions are built.

- **Expressions with a postfix:** These are main expressions that are followed by an operator, such as array subscript or postfix increment.

- **Unary operators are used to creating expressions:** In an expression, unary operators affect just one operand.

- **Binary operators are used to creating expressions:** In an expression, binary operators act on two operands.

- **The conditional operator is used in expressions:** The conditional operator is a ternary operator that accepts three operands and is the only one in C++.

- **Expressions that never change:** Constant expressions are fully made up of constant data.

- **Type conversions are explicit in expressions:** In expressions, explicit type conversions, or "casts", can be employed.

- **Pointer-to-member operators are used in expressions.**

- **Casting:** In expressions, type-safe "casts" can be employed.

- **Information about the type of run-time:** During program execution, determine the type of object.

Primary Expressions

Primary expressions serve as the foundation for more complicated expressions. They can be literals, names, or names with the scope-resolution operator qualified (::).

Syntax:

```
primary-exp
    literal
    this
    name
    :: name ( exp )
```

A literal is a basic expression that never changes. Its type is determined by the way it is specified. See Literals for further information on how to specify literals.

The "This" keyword is a class object reference. It can be accessed using nonstatic member functions. It refers to the class instance for which the function was called. Outside of the body of a class member function, the "this" keyword isn't allowed.

The "this" pointer type is type * const within procedures that don't explicitly change it (where type is the class name). The kinds of this and member function declarations are seen in the following example:

Example:

```cpp
// expre_Primary_Expressions.cpp
class Examp
{
public:
```

```
    void Func();
    void Func() const;
    void Func() volatile;
};
```

See this pointer for additional information on changing the type of "this" pointer.

The main expression is a scope resolution operator (::) followed by a name. These names must be global names, not member names. The statement of the name determines the kind of expression. If the declaring name is a l-value (that is, it may appear on the left-hand side of an assignment expression), it's an l-value. Even though a global name is concealed in the current scope, the scope-resolution operator permits it to be referenced.

The main expression is contained in parenthesis. Its type and value are the same as the unparenthesized expression's type and value. If the unparenthesized expression is an l-value, it's an l-value.

The Following Are Some Examples of Primary Expressions

```
400 // literal
'd' // literal
this // a pointer to the class instance
::func // global function
::operator + // global operator
::B::C // global qualified name
( i + 3 ) // parenthesized exp
```

Variadic Templates and Ellipsis

A variadic template is a class or function template that accepts an unlimited number of arguments. This method is beneficial for C++ library authors since it can be used to create both class and function templates, providing a wide variety of type-safe and non-trivial functionality and flexibility.

Syntax:

Variadic templates employ an ellipsis in two ways. It denotes a parameter pack to the left of the parameter name, and it extends the parameter packs into distinct names to the right of the parameter name.

```
template<typename... Arg> class class-name;
```

Example:

```
#include <iostream>

using namespace std;

void print() {
    cout << endl;
}

template <typename D> void print(const
D& d) {
    cout << d << endl;
}

template <typename First, typename...
Rest> void print(const First& first,
const Rest&... rest) {
    cout << first << ", ";
    print(rest...);
}
```

```
int main()
{
    print(); // calls first overload
    print(1); // calls second overload
    print(20, 30);
    print(200, 300, 400);
    print("second", 3, "fourth", 4.14139);
}
```

Output:

```
1
20, 30
200, 300, 400
second, 3, fourth, 4.14139
```

Postfix Expressions

Primary expressions or expressions in which postfix operators follow a primary expression make up postfix expressions. The following table lists the postfix operators.

Operator Name	Operator Notation
Subscript	[ ]
Function call	( )
Explicit type conversion	*type-name* ( )
Member access	. or ->
Postfix increment	++
Postfix decrement	--

Arguments Both Formal and Informal

In "actual arguments", calling programs send information to called functions. The data is accessed by the called functions using "formal arguments".

When a function is invoked, it performs the following tasks:

All actual arguments (those provided by the caller) are assessed. There is no implied sequence in which these arguments are processed, but before entering the function, all arguments are evaluated and all side effects are finished.

In the expression list, each formal argument is initialized with its real matching parameter. (In the body of a function, a formal argument is one that is defined in the function header and utilized.) Conversions are executed as initialized, with both standard and user-defined conversions used to transform an actual input to the right type. The following code illustrates the initialization process conceptually:

Syntax:

```
void Func (int a) ; // Function
prototype
...
Func (4) ;
```

Example:

```
void func( long para1, double para2 );

int main()
{
    long b = 2;
    double c = 4;

    // func call with actual arguments
    func( b, c );
}
```

```
// func define with formal parameters
void func( long para1, double para2 )
{
}
```

Unary Operators in Expressions

In an expression, unary operators affect just one operand.
The following are the unary operators:

- Indirection operator (*)

- Address-of operator (&)

- Unary plus operator (+)

- Unary negation operator (-)

- Logical negation operator (!)

- One's complement operator (~)

- Prefix increment operator (++)

- Prefix decrement operator (--)

- Cast operator ()

- sizeof operator

- __uuidof operator

- alignof operator

- new operator

- delete operator

Binary Operators in Expressions

In an expression, binary operators act on two operands. The binary operators are as follows:

- Operators that multiply
  - Multiplication (*)
  - Division (/)
  - Modulus (%)
- Operators that additive
  - Addition (+)
  - Subtraction (-)
  - Shift operators
  - Right shift (>>)
  - Left shift (<<)
- Operators that relational and equality
  - Less than (<)
  - Greater than (>)
  - Less than or equal to (<=)
  - Greater than or equal to (>=)
  - Equal to (==)
  - Not equal to (!=)
- Operators that Bitwise
  - Bitwise AND (&)

- Bitwise OR (^)

- Bitwise OR (|)

- Operators that Logical

  - Logical AND (&&)

  - Logical OR (||)

- Assignment operators

  - Assignment (=)

  - Addition (+=)

  - Subtraction (-=)

  - Multiplication (*=)

  - Division (/=)

  - Modulus (%=)

  - Left shift (<<=)

  - Right shift (>>=)

  - Bitwise AND (&=)

  - Bitwise exclusive (^=)

  - Bitwise inclusive (|=)

- Comma Operator (,)

Expressions That Never Change

The term "constant value" refers to a value that does not vary. C++ offers two keywords that allow you to express and enforce the idea that an object is not meant to be changed.

Constant expressions—In C++, constant-evaluating expressions are necessary for declarations of:

- Bounds of an array

- In case of statements, selectors are used

- Specification for the length of a bit-field

- Initializers for enumerations

In constant expressions, only the following operands are permitted:

- Literals

- Constants of enumeration

- Constant expressions are used to initialize values specified as const

- Expressions of sizeof

FOLD EXPRESSIONS

Variadic templates are supported in C++11. These are templates with an unlimited amount of template parameters. A parameter pack stores the arbitrary number. Furthermore, using C++17, we may use a binary operator to decrease a parameter pack directly. As a result, you may use C++ to implement the Haskell functions foldl, foldr, foldl1, and foldr1. Let's have a look at how to turn a list into a value.

Example:

```
#include <iostream>

bool allVar(){
  return true;
}

template<typename C, typename ...Cs>
bool allVar(C c, Cs ... cs){
  return c && allVar(cs...);
}

template<typename... Args>
bool all(Args... args) { return (...
&& args); }

int main(){

  std::cout << std::boolalpha;

  std::cout << "allVar(): " << allVar()
<< std::endl;
  std::cout << "all(): " << all() <<
std::endl;

  std::cout << "allVar(true): " <<
allVar(true) << std::endl;
  std::cout << "all(true): " <<
all(true) << std::endl;

  std::cout << "allVar(true, true,
true, false): " << allVar(true, true,
true, false) << std::endl;
  std::cout << "all(true, true, true,
false): " << all(true, true, true,
false) << std::endl;

}
```

If all arguments are true, both templates allVar and all will return true at compilation time. AllVar uses variadic templates; all variadic templates are combined with fold expressions. To begin, go to allVar. Variable templates use recursion to evaluate their arguments. As a result, if the parameter pack is empty, the function allVar is the boundary condition. The recursion occurs of the function template allVar. The parameter pack is defined by the three dots. Two operations are supported by parameter packs.

Output:

```
allVar(true): true
all(true): true
allVar(true, true, true, false): false
all(true, true, true, false): false
```

There Are Two Options

Now let's look at the two-fold expression variants that result in four different fold expressions. Fold expression might be difficult to understand at first.

There should be a default value. The binary operator determines this value to be decreased from the right to the left.

Between the algorithms allVar and all, there is a slight difference. For the empty parameter pack, all have the default value true.

In fold expressions, C++17 allows 32 binary operators: "+ - * / % ^ & | = < > << >> += -= *= /= %= ^= &= |= <<= >>= == != <= >= && ||, . * ->*".

There are default values for a couple of them:

Operator	Symbol	Default-Value
Logic AND	&&	True
Logic OR	||	False
Comma Operator	,	Void

You must specify an initial value for binary operators that do not have a default value. You can set an initial value for binary operators that have a default value.

The parameter pack will be handled from the left if the ellipsis is to the left of it. The same may be said about right. This is also true if a starting value is provided.

Syntax:

```
template<typename... Args>
bool all(Args... args) { return (true
&& ... && args); }
```

Unary Folds

To fold parameter packs over a specified operator, unary folds are utilised. Unary folds can be divided into two types:

- Unary Left Fold (... op pack) has the following expansion:

Syntax:

```
((Pack1 op Pack2) op ...) op PackN
```

- Right Unary Fold (pack op...) extends as follows:

    Syntax:

    ```
    Pack1 op (... (Pack(N-1) op PackN))
    ```

    Example:

    ```
    template<typename... Ts>
    int sum(Ts... args)
    {
        return (... + args); //Unary left
    fold
        //return (args + ...); //Unary
    right fold

        // The two are equivalent if the
    operator is associative.
        // For +, ((3+2)+1) (left fold) ==
    (3+(2+1)) (right fold)
        // For -, ((3-2)-1) (left fold) !=
    (1-(2-1)) (right fold)
    }

    int result = sum(3, 2, 1);
    ```

Binary Folds

Binary folds are unary folds with an additional parameter.
Binary folds may be divided into two types:

- Binary Left Fold—(value op ... op pack)

    Syntax:

    ```
    (((Value op Pack1) op Pack2) op ...)
    op PackN
    ```

- Binary Right Fold (pack op ... op value)

Syntax:

```
Pack1 op (... op (Pack(N-1) op (PackN
op Value)))
```

Syntax:

```
template<typename... Cs>
int removeFrom(int num, Cs... args)
{
    return (n - ... - args); //Binary
left fold
    // Due to the lack of operator-
associativity, binary right fold
cannot be utilised.
}

int res = removeFrom 2100, 3, 20, 18);
```

Folding Over a Comma

It's not uncommon to need to apply a specific function to each member in a parameter pack. The best we can achieve with C++11 is:

Syntax:

```
template <class... Cs>
void print_all(std::ostream& os, Cs
const&... args) {
    using expander = int[];
    (void)expander{0,
```

```
        (void(os << args), 0)...
    };
}
```

FRIEND KEYWORD

Classes that are well-designed encapsulate their functionality, hiding their implementation while offering a clean, well-documented interface. As long as the interface remains unaltered, this enables redesign or modification.

Multiple classes that rely on each other's implementation details may be necessary for a more complicated scenario. Friend classes and functions allow these peers access to each other's details without endangering the specified interface's encapsulation and hiding information.

Function

Any function that is a buddy of a class or structure can be declared. If a function is a class's buddy, it has access to all of the class's protected and private members:

Example:

```
void friend_function();
void non_friend_function();

class Prihold {
public:
    Prihold(int val) : private_
value(val) {}
private:
    int pri_val;
    // Declare function as a friend.
```

```
    friend void friend_function();
};

void non_friend_function() {
    Prihold ph(30);
    // Compilation error
    std::cout << ph.pri_val <<
std::endl;
}

void friend_function() {
    // OK: friends may access private
values.
    PrivateHolder ph(30);
    std::cout << ph.pri_val <<
std::endl;
}
```

The semantics of friends are unaffected by access modifiers. A friend's public, protected, and private statements are all the same.

Method
```
class Access {
public:
    void private_accesser();
};

class PriHold {
public:
    PriHold(int val) : private_value(val)
{}
    friend void
Accesser::private_accesser();
```

```
private:
    int pri_val;
};

void Accesser::private_accesser() {
    PriHold ph(10);
    std::cout << ph.pri_val << std::endl;
}
```

Friend Class

It is possible to declare a whole class as a friend. A buddy class declaration indicates that every member of the friend has access to the declaring class's secret and protected members:

```
class Access {
public:
    void private_accesser1();
    void private_accesser2();
};

class PriHold {
public:
    PriHold(int val) : private_value(val) {}
    friend class Access;
private:
    int pri_val;
};

void Accesser::private_accesser1() {
    PrivateHolder ph(20);
    // OK.
    std::cout << ph.pri_val << std::endl;
}
```

```
void Accesser::private_accesser2() {
    PriHold ph(20);
    std::cout << ph.pri_val + 1 << std::endl;
}
```

OVERLOADING A FUNCTION

Multiple functions with the same name exist in the same area (known as scope) and differ only in their signature or the arguments they take, known as function overloading.

Syntax:

```
void print(const std::string &str)
{
    std::cout << "This is a string: " <<
str << std::endl;
}
```

In the case of function overloading, the return type is:

A function cannot be overloaded depending on its return type. Consider the following scenario:

Example:

```
std::string getValue()
{
  return "hei";
}

int getValue()
{
  return 0;
}

int y = getValue();
```

OVERLOADING OF FUNCTION TEMPLATES

What Is Legitimate Overloading of a Function Template?

The rules for non-template function overloading (same name, but distinct argument types) may be applied to a function template, and the overloading is valid if.

- The return type is different.

- Except for the naming of parameters and the existence of default arguments, the template parameter list is different.

Comparing two argument types for a regular function is simple for the compiler since it knows all the information. A type within a template, on the other hand, may not have been determined yet. As a result, the estimated rule for when two parameter types are equal is that non-dependent types and values must match, and dependent types and expressions must have the exact spelling, except for template parameters, which may be renamed. If, however, two values inside the types are regarded distinct under such varied spellings yet always instantiate to the same values, the overloading is incorrect, but no compiler diagnostic is necessary.

Syntax:

```
template<typename T>
void f(T*) { }

template<typename T>
void f(T) { }
```

FUTURES AND PROMISES

Promises and Futures are used to transfer a single item between threads.

- The thread that generates the result sets a std::promise object.

- A std::future object can be used to get a value, test for availability, or pause execution until the value is available.

- **std::promise and std::future**

The example below creates a promise that another thread will consume:

Example:

```
{
        auto pro = std::promise<std::
string>();

        auto prod = std::thread([&]
        {
            promise.set_value("Hello
Everyone");
        });

        auto fut = promise.get_future();

        auto cons = std::thread([&]
        {
            std::cout << future.get();
        });
```

```
        prod.join();
        cons.join();
}
```

- **std::future and std::packaged_task**

  std::packaged task combines a
  function with its return type's
  associated promise:

  Example:

  ```
  template<typename F>
  auto async_deferred(F&& func) ->
  std::future<decltype(func())>
  {
      auto tas   = std::packaged_
  task<decltype(func())()>(std::forwar
  d<F>(function));
      auto fut = task.get_future();

      std::thread(std::move(task)).
  detach();

      return std::move(fut);
  }
  ```

The thread immediately begins to run. We may either remove it or have it join the scope at the end. The result is ready when the std::thread function call completes.

- **std::future_errc and std::future_error:** If the std::promise and std::future restrictions are not satisfied, a std::future_error exception is produced.

The error code component of the exception is of type std::future_errc, and its values, as well as certain test cases, are as follows:

Example:

```
enum class fut_errc {
    broken_promise          = /*
task is no longer shared */,
    future_already_retrieved  = /*
answer was already retrieved */,
    promise_already_satisfied = /*
answer was stored already */,
    no_state                = /*
access to a promise in non-shared
state */
};
```

- **Inactive promise:**

  Example:

```
int tt()
{
    std::promise<int> pr;
    return 0;
}
```

- **Unused active promise:**

```
int t()
    {
        std::promise<int> pr;
```

```
        auto futu = pr.get_future();
//blocks
        return 0;
    }
```

- **std::async and std::future:** std::async is used to initiate several parallel merge_sort processes in the following naïve parallel merge sort example. std::future is used to synchronize and wait for results:

Example:

```
#include <iostream>
using namespace std;

void merge(int low,int mid,int high,
vector<int>&num)
{
    vector<int> copy(num.size());
    int a,b,c,d;
    a=low;
    b=low;
    c=mid+1;

    while((a<=mid)&&(c<=high))
    {
        if(num[a]<=num[j])
        {
            copy[b]=num[a];
            h++;
        }
        else
        {
```

```cpp
                copy[b]=num[c];
                c++;
            }
            b++;
        }
        if(a>mid)
        {
            for(d=c;d<=high;d++)
            {
                copy[b]=num[d];
                b++;
            }
        }
        else
        {
            for(d=a;d<=mid;d++)
            {
                copy[b]=num[d];
                i++;
            }
        }
        for(d=low;d<=high;d++)
            swap(num[d],copy[d]);
}

void merge_sort(int low,int
high,vector<int>& num)
{
    int mid;
    if(low<high)
    {
        mid = low + (high-low)/2;
        auto fut1   = std::async(s
td::launch::deferred, [&]()
```

```
                {
                merge_sort(low,mid,num);
                });
        auto fut2    = std::async(s
td::launch::deferred, [&]()
                {
                merge_sort(mid+1,high,
num) ;
                });

        fut1.get();
        fut2.get();
        merge(low,mid,high,num);
    }
}
```

Classes for Asynchronous Operations

- **std::async:** is used to conduct asynchronous operations

- **std::future:** gives you access to an asynchronous operation's outcome

- The outcome of an asynchronous operation is packaged with **std::promise**

- **std::packaged_task** combines a function with its return type's corresponding promise

C++ HIGHER ORDER FUNCTIONS

Functions that take functions as input are known as higher-order functions. It's used in functional languages that aren't utilized in C++, however, that's slowly changing now that C++11 has lambdas and std::function… and many people are unaware that "std::function" is not a tool that can be used in all situations. We'll show you how to provide a function as a parameter to a separate calling function. The general-purpose algorithms std::transform() and std::accumulate() have been used in numerous examples throughout this book, such as creating string utilities to produce uppercase or lowercase copies of a string or summing the values of a range. These are essentially higher-order function implementations that map and fold. A higher-order function takes one or more other functions as parameters and uses them to produce a new collection of data or a value from a set of data (a list, vector, map, tree, and so on). We'll explore how to use C++ standard containers to implement map and fold methods in this recipe.

Syntax:

```
return_type func_name(func<return_type
fun_name(arg_list), other function
args)
```

Function name accepts a function named fun name as an argument in the example above. Additional parameters can be sent to both function name and fun name.

Example:

```
#include <bits/stdc++.h>
using namespace std;

// The function that will be provided
to the calling function as an argument
bool Parser(string y)
{
```

```
    // Check if string start
    // with alphabet 'P'
    return y[0] == 'P';
}

vector<string> Parse(vector<string> b,
                function<bool(string)>
Parser)
{
    vector<string> ans;

    // Traverse the vector a
    for (auto str : b) {
        if (Parser(str)) {
            ans.push_back(str);
        }
    }

    // Return the resultant vector
    return ans;
}

// Driver Code
int main()
{
    vector<string> dict = { "hello",
"hoop",
                        "Hii", "for" };

    // Function Call for Higher
    // Functions Order
    vector<string> ans = Parse(dict,
Parser);
```

```
// Results print
for (auto str : ans) {
    cout << str << " ";
}

return 0;
}
```

Output:

```
Hoop Hii
```

Higher-Order Functions Provide the Following Advantages

Many issues may be solved by employing the higher-order function. For example, create a function that takes a list and another function as input and applies the second function to each item of the list before returning the new list. This may be easily accomplished in Haskell by utilizing the built-in higher-order function map. The map's definition is as follows:

Syntax:

```
map :: (c -> d) -> [c] -> [d]
map _ [ ] = [ ]
map f (y : ys) = f x : map f ys
```

The Function Initialization Is the First Line

"Is of the type" is represented by the symbol of the element.

[c] represents a list of similar elements written by the entity after the last -> is always the function's return type.

In Haskell, a function always returns just one object.

(c->d) is a function that goes from c to d. We defined the map using recurrence, with [] being an empty list and denoting "anything".

The second line shows that if an empty list and any function are both supplied, the result will be an empty list.

IMPLEMENTATION MAP

A Map is a type of associative container that stores items in a mapped order. There is a key value and a mapped value for each element. The key values of two mapped values cannot be the same.

Here are the functions that are used:

If the element with key value "b" in the map is discovered, m::find() provides an iterator to it, else it returns the iterator to end.

- **m::erase():** Removes the map's key value.

- **m:: equal range():** Returns a list of pairs as an iterator. The pair refers to the limits of a range containing all of the container's components with a key equivalent to a key.

- **m insert():** This function is used to insert elements into the map container.

- **m size():** The number of items in the map container is returned by m size().

- **m count():** Returns the number of matches to an element in the map with the key value "a" or "f".

Example:

```
#include<iostream>
#include <map>
#include <string>
using namespace std;
int main () {
    map<char, int> m;
    map<char, int>::iterator it;
    m.insert (pair<char, int>('a', 20));
    m.insert (pair<char, int>('b', 30));
    m.insert (pair<char, int>('c', 40));
    m.insert (pair<char, int>('d', 50));
    cout<<"Size of the map: "<< m.size()
<<endl;
    cout << "map contains:\n";
    for (it = m.begin(); it != m.end();
++it)
        cout << (*it).first << " => " <<
(*it).second << '\n';
    for (char c = 'a'; c <= 'd'; c++) {
        cout << "There is " << m.count(c)
<< " element with key " << c << ":";
        map<char, int>::iterator it;
        for (it = m.equal_range(c).first;
it != m.equal_range(c).second; ++it)
            cout << ' ' << (*it).second;
            cout << endl;
    }
    if (m.count('a'))
        cout << "The key a is present\n";
    else
        cout << "The key a is not
present\n";
    if (m.count('f'))
```

```
        cout << "The key f is present\n";
    else
        cout << "The key f is not
present\n";
    it = m.find('b');
    m.erase (it);
    cout<<"Size of the map: "<<m.
size()<<endl;
    cout << "map contains:\n";
    for (it = m.begin(); it != m.end();
++it)
    cout << (*it).first << " => " <<
(*it).second << '\n';
    return 0;
}
```

Output:

```
Size of the map: 4
map contains:
a => 20
b => 30
c => 40
d => 50
There is 1 element with key a: 20
There is 1 element with key b: 30
There is 1 element with key c: 40
There is 1 element with key d: 50
The key a is present
The key f is not present
Size of the map: 3
Map contains:
a => 20
c => 40
d => 50
```

This brings us to the end of this chapter.

In this chapter we have learned about Defaulted and Deleted Functions, as well as Lambdas and Standard Algorithms, in this chapter. We also learned how to Write a Function Template with a Variable of Number of Arguments and how to Simplify Variadic Function Templates using Fold Expressions.

CHAPTER 5

Memory Management in C++

IN THIS CHAPTER

- ➢ Computer Memory
- ➢ Process Memory
- ➢ Objects in Memory
- ➢ Custom Memory Management

In this chapter, we'll study what memory management is and why it's essential, as well as what memory management operators are and why they're helpful. Furthermore, we will learn what dynamic memory allocation is, how to

DOI: 10.1201/9781003214762-5

allocate memory dynamically, and why memory management is essential. What are objects' new and delete operators? In addition, we will learn about memory objects and custom memory.

A logical grouping of statements that execute a given purpose is called a function. You may avoid writing the same code for different input values within the program by introducing a function. To conduct the action, all you have to do is call the function.

- **Return type:** This specifies the type of value that the function will return as an output. Integer, character, and other return types are possible. A function does not always have to return a value. You can define the function with a void return type in this instance.

- **Function name:** The function's name, for instance, foo. This name can be used to invoke the function from anywhere inside the program's scope.

- **Function parameters:** Variables containing the argument values given when the function is invoked are function parameters.

MEMORY MANAGEMENT

In C++, we may allocate memory for a variable or an array during runtime. Dynamic memory allocation is the term for this. The compiler controls the memory assigned to variables in other programming languages, such as Java and Python. In C++, however, this is not the case.

After we do not need a variable in C++, we must manually deallocate the dynamically created memory. Using the new and delete operators, we may dynamically allocate and subsequently deallocate memory.

What Is the Purpose of Memory Management?

Because arrays contain homogenous data, memory is allocated to the array when it is declared most of the time. When the precise memory is not specified until runtime, a problem might emerge. We declare an array with a limit size to avoid this issue, but some memory will be unused. To prevent memory waste, we utilize the new operator to allocate memory during runtime dynamically.

Operators for Memory Management

In C, the malloc() and calloc() functions are used to allocate memory at runtime, whereas the free () function is used to deallocate dynamically generated memory. These functions are also available in C++, although unary operators such as new and delete are defined to do the same job, namely allocating and freeing memory.

THE NEW OPERATOR'S BENEFITS

The new operator has the following advantages over the malloc() function:

- It does not need the size of() operator since the size of the data object is calculated automatically.

- It does not necessary to employ typecasting because it delivers the right data type pointer.

- The new and delete operators, like other operators, can be overloaded.

- It also lets you initialize the data object while it's being built in memory.

NEW OPERATOR IN C++

The new operator gives a variable memory. As an example,

```
// declare a reference to an int
int* pointerVar;
// allocate memory dynamically
pointerVar = new int;
// assign a value to the memory that has
been allocated
*pointerVar = 55;
```

Using the new operator, we have dynamically allocated memory for an int variable.

We allocated memory dynamically using the reference pntVar. Because the new operator returns the memory location's address, this is the case. When dealing with an array, the new operator returns the address of the array's first element.

The syntax for employing the new operator may be seen in the example above:

```
pointerVar = new dataType;
```

DELETE OPERATOR

We can deallocate the memory held by a variable that we have declared dynamically after requiring it. The delete operator is used for this. Memory deallocation refers to the process of returning memory to the operating system.

This operator's syntax is as follows:

```
delete pointerVar;
```

Example:
```
// declare a reference to an int
int* pointVari;
// allocate memory dynamically
pointVari = new int;
// assign value to the variable memory
*pointVari = 55;
// print the value stored in memory
cout << *pointVari;
// deallocate the memory
delete pointVari;
```

Using the pointer pointVari, we have dynamically allocated memory for an int variable.

Is It Permissible for a Member Function to Tell You to Remove Something?

- You must be sure that this object was allocated using new (not new[], placement new, a local object on the stack, a namespace-scope/global, or a member of another object; but just new).

- You must be confident that your member function will be the very last member function called on this object.

- You must be sure that the remainder of your member function (after the delete this line) does not come into contact with any part of this object. This includes code that will execute in destructors for any still-alive objects allocated on the stack.

- You must be very specific that no one touches this pointer after you delete this line. To put it another way, you can't look at it, compare it to another pointer, compare it to nullptr, print it, cast it, or do anything with it.

Allocating Memory in a Dynamic Way

A simple memory architecture utilized by each C++ software is shown below:

- **Code segment:** This is where the compiled program containing executive instructions is saved. It is a read-only document. The code portion is put behind the stack and heap to avoid overwriting them.

- **Data segment:** This is where global variables and static variables are maintained. It isn't just for reading.

- **Stack:** A stack is a type of memory that has been pre-allocated. A LIFO data structure is a stack. The stack is pushed up with each new variable. Memory is released when a variable is no longer in scope. When a stack variable is removed, the memory space it used becomes accessible for other variables. As functions push and pop local variables, the stack expands and contracts. It keeps track of local data, return addresses, arguments provided to functions, and memory status.

- **Heap:** Memory is allocated while the application is running. Memory is allocated using the new operator, whereas memory is dealt with using the delete operator.

Source Code:

```cpp
#include <iostream>
using namespace std;
int main() {
    // int pointer declaration
    int* pntInt;
    // declare float
    float* pntFloat;
    // allocate memory dynamically
    pntInt = new int;
    pntFloat = new float;
    // value assigning to the memory
    *pntInt = 55;
    *pntFloat = 55.55f;
    cout << *pntInt << endl;
    cout << *pntFloat << endl;
    // deallocate memory
    delete pntInt;
    delete pntFloat;
    return 0;
}
```

Output:

```
55
55.55
```

Arrays' New and Delete Operators

Source Code:

```
// GPA of several students is stored
and shown in this program where n is
the num of students entered

#include <iostream>
using namespace std;

int main() {
    int numb;
    cout << "Enter total number of
students: ";
    cin >> numb;
    float* pntr;

    // memory allocation
    pntr = new float[numb];

    cout << "Enter GPA" << endl;
    for (int c = 0; c < numb; ++c) {
        cout << "Student" << c + 1 <<
": ";
        cin >> *(pntr + c);
    }

    cout << "\nDisplaying GPA" << endl;
    for (int c = 0; c < numb; ++c) {
        cout << "Student" << c + 1 <<
" :" << *(pntr + c) << endl;
    }
```

```
    // ptr memory is released
    delete[] pntr;

    return 0;
}
```

Output:

```
Enter total number of students: 5
Enter GPA
Student1: 4.4
Student2: 5
Student3: 3
Student4: 7
Student5: 8

Displaying GPA
Student1: 4.4
Student2: 5
Student3: 3
Student4: 7
Student5: 8
```

In this application, the user enters the number of students and saves it in the numb variable, and then we dynamically allocate memory for the float array using new.

We use pointer notation to insert data into the array (and eventually output it).

We use the code delete[] pntr; to deallocate the array memory when we no longer require it.

Use [] after delete. To indicate that the memory deallocation is for an array, we use square brackets [].

Objects' New and Delete Operators

Source Code:

```cpp
#include <iostream>
using namespace std;

class Stud {
    int age;

  public:

    // constructor initializes age
    Stud() : age(10) {}

    void getAge() {
        cout << "Age: " << age << endl;
    }
};

int main() {

    // declare Student object
dynamically
    Stud* pntr = new Stud();

    // call getAge()
    pntr->getAge();

    // released ptr memory
    delete pntr;

    return 0;
}
```

Output:

```
Age: 10
```

We've built a Stud class with a private variable age in this application.

In the default function Stud(), we set the age to 10 and use the method getAge to report its result (). In main(), we use the new operator to construct a Student object and the pointer pntr to refer to its address.

The Stud() function sets the age to 10 as soon as the object is created.

IN C++, MALLOC() VS NEW

In C++, both malloc() and new are used for the same thing. At runtime, they are utilized to allocate memory. Malloc() and new, on the other hand, have distinct syntax. The significant distinction between malloc() and new is that new is an operator, whereas malloc() is a predefined standard library function in a stdlib header file.

So, What's New?

The new is a memory allocation operator that is used at runtime to allocate memory. The heap stores the memory allocated by the new operator. It returns the memory's beginning address, which is then assigned to the variable. The new operator in C++ works similarly to the malloc() function in the C programming language. Although the malloc() method is compatible with C++, the new operator is more commonly employed because of its benefits.

Syntax:

```
type variable = new
type(parameter_list);
```

- **type:** This specifies the datatype of the variable for which the new operator is allocating memory.

- **variable:** The name of the variable that points to the memory is variable.

- **parameter_list:** The parameter list is a list of initialized values for a variable.

The sizeof() operator is not used by the new operator to allocate memory. It also avoids using the resize operator because the new operator creates enough memory for an object. It's a construct that invokes the function to initialize an object at the moment of declaration.

Because the new operator allocates memory in a heap, an exception is thrown if it is not available when the new operator tries to assign it. The application will be terminated unexpectedly if our code is unable to handle the exception.

Example:

```
#include <iostream>
using namespace std;
int main()
{
 int *pntr; // integer pointer
 pntr=new int; // allocating memory
```

```
std::cout << "Enter number: " <<
std::endl;
std::cin >>*pntr;
std::cout << "Entered number"
<<*pntr<< std::endl;
return 0;
}
```

Output:
```
Enter number:
30
Entered number 30
```

What Exactly Is Malloc()?

A malloc() function is a runtime memory allocation function. This method returns a void pointer, which may be given to any kind of pointer. This void pointer can be typecast to get a pointer that refers to a specific type of memory.

The malloc syntax is as follows:

```
type vari_name = (type *)
malloc(sizeof(type));
```

Because heap memory is utilized to meet all dynamic memory requirements, the realloc() function might increase the memory if sufficient memory is not available. The malloc() function returns a reference to memory allocated in a heap. The heap memory is restricted, our code detects that it is in use when it starts running. It uses the free() function to release the memory when it has finished its task. After it completes its work, it frees the memory using the free() method. When code attempts to use memory that isn't accessible, the malloc() function returns a NULL pointer.

The free() function can be used to deallocate memory allocated by the malloc() method.

Example:

```cpp
#include <iostream>
#include<stdlib.h>
using namespace std;

int main()
{

  int ln;   // declaration variable
  std::cout << "Enter the count:" <<
std::endl;
  std::cin >> ln;
  int *pntr; // pointer variable
declaration
  pntr=(int*) malloc(sizeof(int)*ln);
// allocating memory
  for(int c=0;c<ln;c++)
  {
      std::cout << "Enter num : " <<
std::endl;
      std::cin >> *(pntr+c);
  }
  std::cout << "Entered elements: " <<
std::endl;
    for(int c=0;c<ln;c++)
  {
     std::cout << *(pntr+c) << std::endl;
  }
free(pntr);
    return 0;
}
```

Output:

```
Enter the count:
5
Enter num:
12
Enter num:
5
Enter num:
7
Enter num:
9
Enter num:
8
Entered elements:
12
5
7
9
8
```

Differences Between Malloc() and New()?

- The new operator generates an object by calling the procedure, but the malloc() method does not. The function is called by the new operator, whereas the destructor is called by the delete operator to destroy the object. The most important contrast between malloc() and new is this.

- Malloc() is a predefined function in the stdlib header file, while new is an operator.

- Overloading the new operator is possible, but not with the malloc() function.

- If there isn't enough memory in a heap, the new operator will throw an exception, and the malloc() method will return a NULL pointer.

- We must specify the number of objects to be allocated in the new operator, while we must specify the number of bytes to be allocated in the malloc() function.

- To deallocate memory in the event of a new operator, we must utilize the delete operator. However, in the malloc() method, we must deallocate the memory using the free() function.

Syntax:

```
type reference_vari = new type name;
```

Example:

```
int *b;
p = (int *) malloc(sizeof(int))
```

The above line allocates memory on a heap for an integer variable and then saves the address of the reserved memory in the "b" variable.

- The memory allocated using the malloc() method may be freed with the free() function.

- The memory can't be expanded after it's been allocated with the new operator. On the other hand, the memory is allocated using the malloc() method and subsequently reallocated using the realloc() function.

- Because new is a construct and malloc is a function, new takes less time to execute than malloc().

- The address of the newly formed object is returned by the new operator, not the distinct pointer variable. The malloc() method, on the other hand, returns a void pointer that may be typecast into any type.

PROCESS MEMORY

A process is a runnable programme that is loaded into memory. A method is just a running program.

When a program is generated, it is nothing more than a collection of bytes saved on the hard disc as a passive object. When a program is double-clicked on Windows or the name of the executable file is entered on the command line, the program begins loading in memory and becomes an active entity.

Operating System Memory Management

Memory management is a component of the operating system that regulates or maintains primary memory and moves processes from the main memory to the disc during execution. Memory management maintains track of every memory location, whether it's in use or not. It determines how much memory should be allotted to each process. It specifies which methods will be allocated memory and when they will be given memory. It monitors when memory is freed or unallocated and adjusts the state accordingly.

Memory may be defined as a collection of data in a certain format. It's utilized to keep track of instructions and data that have been processed. A vast array or set of words or bytes makes up the memory, each with its place. A computer system's principal goal is to run programs. During execution, these programs and the data they access should reside in the main memory. The CPU retrieves instructions from memory based on the program counter value.

What Is Main Memory?

A modern computer's main memory is critical to its functionality. A vast array of words or bytes, ranging in size from hundreds of thousands to billions, is referred to as main memory. The CPU and I/O devices share main memory, which is a store of quickly accessible information. When the CPU is actively using programs and data, they are stored in the main memory. Because main memory is linked to the CPU, transferring instructions and data in and out of the processor is lightning fast.

RAM stands for random access memory. This memory is a volatile memory, which means it may be erased at any time. When there is a power outage, the data in RAM is last.

What Is Memory Management?

In a multiprogramming computer, the operating system takes up a portion of memory, while other processes rest. The process of assigning memory to various uses is known as memory management. Memory management is a mechanism used by operating systems to coordinate actions between the main memory and the disc while running. The fundamental objective of memory management is to achieve practical usage of memory.

Why Is Memory Management Necessary?

- Before and after the procedure, allocate and de-allocate memory

- To keep track of how much memory is being utilized by processes

- To keep fragmentation to a minimum

- To make the most use of the main memory

- To keep data safe while the procedure is running

Space for Logical and Physical Addresses

- **Space for logical addresses:** The term "logical address" refers to an address created by the CPU. A virtual address is another name for it. The size of the process can be described as the logical address space. It is possible to modify a logical address.

- **Physical Address space:** A "Physical Address" is an address viewed by the memory unit (i.e. one that is loaded into the memory's memory address register). A Real address is the same as a physical address.

Physical address space is the collection of all physical addresses that correspond to these logical addresses. Memory Management Unit (MMU) generates a physical address. A hardware component known as a MMU performs the run-time mapping from virtual to physical locations. The physical address is always the same.

Loading Methods: Static and Dynamic

A loader loads a process into the main memory in two ways: static and dynamic. Loading can be divided into two categories:

- **Static loading:** Static loading is when the complete program is loaded into a single address. It necessitates additional memory.

- **Dynamic loading:** The whole program and its data must be in physical memory for a process to operate. As a result, the size of a function is restricted by the amount of physical memory available. Dynamic loading is utilized to ensure optimal memory use. In dynamic loading, a procedure is not loaded until it is called.

Linking, Both Static and Dynamic

A linker is used to conduct static and dynamic linking tasks. A linker is a software that merges several object files created by a compiler into a single executable file.

- **Static linking:** The linker merges all essential software modules into a single executable program via static linking. As a result, there isn't any runtime dependence. Some operating systems only allow static linking, which treats system language libraries like any other object module.

- **Dynamic linking:** Dynamic linking is comparable to dynamic loading in terms of its core principle. For each suitable library routine reference, "Stub" is included in dynamic linking. A stub is a chunk of code that is only a few lines long. When the stub is run, it checks to see if the required procedure is already present in memory. If the routine is not accessible, the software loads it into memory.

SWAPPING

A process must have resided in memory when it is run. Swapping temporarily moves a process from main memory to secondary memory, which is faster than secondary memory. More operations may be executed and fit into memory at the same time, thanks to swapping. The transferred time is the most critical aspect of swapping, and the overall time is proportional to the quantity of memory swapped. Because if a higher priority process requests service, the memory manager can swap out the lower priority process and then load and run the higher priority process, swapping is also known as roll-out, roll-in. After completing the higher priority activity, the lower priority process swapped back into memory and resumed the execution process.

CONTIGUOUS MEMORY ALLOCATION

The main memory should be accessible to both the operating system and the numerous client programs. As a result, memory allocation in the operating system becomes an essential activity. Memory is usually partitioned into two parts: the resident operating system and user processes. Many user processes must be retained in memory at the same time in most instances. As a result, we must examine how to assign available memory to the processes waiting to be brought into memory from the input queue. Each process in neighboring memory allotment is housed in a single contiguous memory segment.

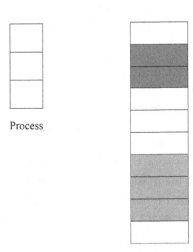

Process

Memory Blocks

Memory Allocation

Memory allocation must be allocated efficiently to achieve optimal memory utilization. Divide memory into numerous fixed-size divisions, each containing precisely one process, is one of the simplest ways for allocating memory. The number of divisions determines the degree of multiprogramming.

Multiple Partition Allocation

A process is chosen from the input queue and loaded into a free partition in this approach. The division becomes accessible for other functions after the process finishes.

Fixed Partition Allocation

In this technique, the operating system keeps track of which sections of memory are free and used up by processes. All memory is initially available for user processes and is treated as a single giant block of memory. The available memory is referred to as a "Hole". When a new process that requires memory, we look for a large enough hole to store it. If the need is met, we allocate RAM to process it; otherwise, the remaining memory is kept accessible for future requests.

When allocating memory, dynamic storage allocation difficulties might arise, such as meeting a request of size n from a list of available holes. There are a few options for dealing with this issue:

First Fit

In this case, the first accessible free slot satisfies the process's criteria.

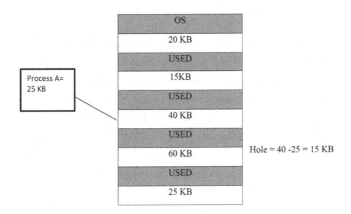

Because the previous two memory blocks did not have enough memory space, the first available free hole in this diagram is a 40 KB memory block that can hold process A (size of 25 KB).

Best Fit

Assign the smallest hole that is large enough to process requirements for the optimum fit. Unless the list is sorted by size, we search the entire list for this.

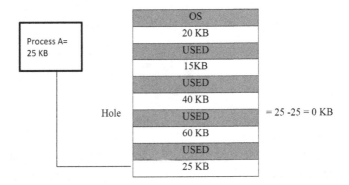

Worst Fit

In the worst-case scenario, process the most enormous available hole. This approach yields the most significant remaining hole.

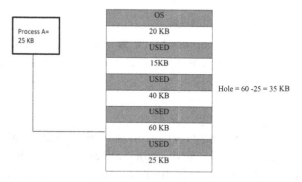

Process A (size 25 KB) is allocated to the most significant available memory block of 60 KB in this case. In the worst-case scenario, inefficient memory use is a big concern.

FRAGMENTATION

A Fragmentation is described as a tiny free hole created when a process is loaded and deleted from memory after execution. These holes can't be allocated to new techniques since they're not merged or don't meet the process's memory requirements. We must decrease memory waste or fragmentation to accomplish a degree of multiprogramming. There are two forms of fragmentation in operating systems:

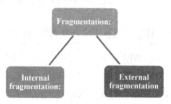

Internal Fragmentation

Internal fragmentation happens when the process is given more memory blocks than requested. As a result, some space remains, resulting in internal fragmentation.

External Fragmentation

We have a free memory block in external fragmentation, but we can't allocate it to process since the blocks aren't contiguous.

PAGING

Paging is a memory management method that eliminates the need for physical memory allocation in contiguous blocks. This technique allows a process's physical address space to be non-contiguous.

- **Logical address:** A logical address, sometimes known as a virtual address, is created by the CPU.

- **Logical address space:** The collection of all logical addresses created by a program is the logical address space or virtual address space.

- **Physical address:** An address that can be found on a memory unit.

- **Physical address space:** The collection of all physical addresses that correlate to logical addresses.

WHAT ARE OBJECTS IN MEMORY?

Above the bar, programs get storage in-memory objects, which are virtual storage chunks. The system divides a memory object into virtual segments, each one a megabyte in size and starting on a megabyte boundary. A memory object might be as large as your installation's memory limitations or as tiny as one megabyte.

A program specifies a location where the system should return the memory object's low address when it creates a memory object. You may think of the address as the memory object's name. The application can use the storage in the memory object the same way it used storage in the 2-gigabyte address space after generating it; see using a memory object. The software is unable to work with storage regions that span several memory objects.

A program can alert the system to its usage of some physical pages that back ranges of addresses in-memory objects, making them accessible for the system to steal and later return. This helps the system manage the physical pages that back ranges of addresses in-memory objects.

The software can release physical pages that have memory object back ranges and, if desired, clear those ranges to zeros. The software can then request that the system return the physical backup from auxiliary storage. When the software no longer needs the memory item, it completely frees it.

OBJECT IN C++

In C++, an object is a physical object such as a chair, automobile, pen, phone, laptop, etc.

An object is a state-and-behavior entity, to put it another way. In this context, the terms "state" and "behaviour" are interchangeable.

A runtime entity is produced during runtime.

A class instance is referred to as an object. The object may be used to access all of the class's members.

Syntax:

```
Class c1;
```

CUSTOM MEMORY MANAGEMENT

When memory blocks are required during runtime, it is necessary. You may have used standard library methods such as malloc and free to dynamically allocate memory from the heap for your application in C and C++. The application then uses this memory for a specific purpose. The goal is usually to add a node to a data structure. To get the memory for a new object in object-oriented languages, dynamic memory allocation is employed.

It's a common misconception that heap will always meet our memory requirements. However, heap has a limit. The physical limit may be evident to most of us, but there is also a subtle "virtual" limit. This constraint becomes more apparent when we use a lot of allocation and deallocation in a long-running application. There is a penalty even while we have complete freedom to return memory to the heap when it is no longer required. Where previously allocated memory has been returned between blocks of memory still in use, the heap may develop "holes".

Our memory allocator would have to seek a new request among the free holes for the suitable "hole" (i.e. large enough to satisfy our demand). Consider a case in which we may not find a large enough hole, but there is plenty of open space. Confused?

Because we want a continuous memory block, none of the holes may be large enough; instead, there may be an excessive number of tiny holes. One of the most significant issues with dynamic memory allocation is memory fragmentation.

A variety of approaches are employed to reduce fragmentation, such as adopting a suitable memory allocation strategy or merging small holes into larger ones. It motivates us to create a bespoke memory manager in which we have total control over the allocation scheme and other ways of dealing with such issues.

But hold on a second. Why can't C and C++'s default memory allocators save us? Let's get into the specifics to address this question.

- The malloc and new are examples of general-purpose memory allocators. Although our code is single-threaded, the malloc function to which it is connected may also handle multithreaded paradigms. This added functionality harms the performance of these procedures.

- The malloc and new, in turn, make memory demands to the operating system kernel, whereas free and delete make memory release requests. This implies that the operating system must transition between user-space and kernel code whenever a memory request is caused because of the frequent context switching; programs that make repeated calls to malloc or new ultimately become sluggish.

- Memory allocated in a program but not used is frequently left undeleted accidentally, and C/C++ does not allow for automated garbage collection. The program's memory footprint grows as a result of this. Because accessible memory becomes increasingly scarce and hard-disk operations are time-consuming, performance suffers significantly in extensive programs.

CUSTOM MEMORY ALLOCATION

Memory leak detection and fast memory allocations can have a significant influence on game speed. The malloc and new are two well-known C++ methods for allocating dynamic (heap) memory; however, because they're general-purpose functions, they're generally sluggish, and some implementations need a context transfer from user mode to kernel mode. These functions also don't come with a built-in memory leak detection mechanism. We can have well-defined use patterns and improve the allocation process using custom allocators. For decades, dynamic memory allocation has been an integral element of most computer systems.

SMART POINTERS AND MEMORY MANAGEMENT

- **RAII and Reference Counting:** Reference counting is a notion that should be familiar to programmers who are familiar with Objective-C/Swift/JavaScript. To prevent memory leaks, the reference count is kept track of. The main concept is to count how many dynamically allocated objects there are. The reference count of the referenced object is increased once every time you add a reference to it. The reference count is decremented by one every time a reference is removed. The pointed heap memory is automatically erased when an object's reference count is decreased to zero. It is not necessarily a great practice in conventional C++ to "remember" to manually release resources.

So, for an object, we usually apply for space when the function is called, and release space when the destructor (called after exiting the scope) is invoked. That example, the RAII resource acquisition is sometimes referred to as the initialization technique.

Everything has exceptions; therefore we must always assign objects to free storage. To "remember" to release resources in conventional C++, we must utilize new and delete. Smart pointers are introduced in C++11, and they use the notion of reference counting to eliminate the need for programmers to manually release memory. These smart pointers need the header file ory>, and include std::shared ptr/std::unique ptr/std::weak ptr.

- **std::shared_ptr:** std::shared_ptr is a smart pointer that keeps track of how many shared ptr refers to an object, obviating the need for the call delete, which deletes the object when the reference count reaches zero.

  However, this is insufficient since std::shared_ ptr must still be called with new, resulting in some imbalance in the code.

  To avoid the usage of new, std::make shared can be used instead. std::make shared will allocate the objects in the given arguments. This object type's std::shared_ptr reference is returned.

Example:

```
#include <iostream>
#include <memory>
void foo(std::shared_ptr<int> j)
{
(*j)++;
}
int main() {
// auto pointer = new int(20); //
illegal, no direct assignment
// Constructed a std::shared_ptr

auto pointer = std::make_
shared<int>(20); foo(pointer);
std::cout << *pointer << std::endl;
// before leaving the scope the
shared_ptr will be destructed
return 0;
}
```

The get() function of std::shared ptr may be used to obtain the raw pointer, and the reset() method can be used to lower the reference count (). Use use count to see an object's reference count ().

Example:

```
auto pointer =
std::make_shared<int>(20);
auto pointer3 = pointer;
auto pointer4 = pointer;

int *g = pointer.get(); // no
increase of reference count
```

```
std::cout << "pointer.use_count() =
" << pointer.use_count() <<
std::endl;
std::cout << "pointer3.use_count() =
" << pointer3.use_count() <<
std::endl;
std::cout << "pointer4.use_count() =
" << pointer4.use_count() <<
std::endl;

pointer3.reset();
std::cout << "reset pointer3:" <<
std::endl;
std::cout << "pointer.use_count() =
" << pointer.use_count() <<
std::endl;
std::cout << "pointer3.use_count() =
" << pointer2.use_count() <<
std::endl;
std::cout << "pointer4.use_count() =
" << pointer3.use_count() <<
std::endl;

pointer4.reset();
std::cout << "reset pointer4:" <<
std::endl;
std::cout << "pointer.use_count() =
" << pointer.use_count() <<
std::endl;
std::cout << "pointer3.use_count() =
" << pointer2.use_count() <<
std::endl;
std::cout << "pointer4.use_count() =
" << pointer3.use_count() <<
std::endl;
```

- **std::unique_ptr:** The exclusive smart pointer std::unique_ptr prevents other smart pointers from sharing the same object, keeping the code safe:

```
std::unique_ptr<int> pointer =
std::make_unique<int>(20);
std::unique_ptr<int> pointer3 = pointer;
```

It's not difficult to use std::make_unique doesn't exist in C++11. make_unique, which may be used on its own:

```
template<typename D, typename ...Args>
std::unique_ptr<D> make_unique( Args&&
...args ) {
return std::unique_ptr<D>( new D(
std::forward<Args>(args)... ) );
}
```

It can't be duplicated since it's monopolized, in other words. We may, however, use std::move to relocate it to another unique_ptr, such as:

```
#include <iostream>
#include <memory>

struct Foo
{
Foo() { std::cout << "Foo::Foo" <<
std::endl;
}
~Foo() { std::cout << "Foo::~Foo" <<
std::endl; }
void foo()
{
std::cout << "Foo::foo" << std::endl;
  }
};
```

```cpp
void f(const Foo &) {
std::cout << "f(const Foo&)" <<
std::endl;
}

int main() {
std::unique_ptr<Foo>
p1(std::make_unique<Foo>());

if (c1) c1->foo();
{
std::unique_ptr<Foo> c2(std::move(c1));

f(*c2);

if(c2) c2->foo();

if(c1) c1->foo(); c1 = std::move(c2);

if(c2) c2->foo();
std::cout << "c2 was destroyed" <<
std::endl;
}

if (c1) c1->foo();

}
```

- **std::weak_ptr:** If you closely consider std::shared_ptr, you will notice that there is still a problem with resources not being released. Consider the following scenario:

```cpp
#include <iostream>
#include <memory>

class C;
class D;
```

```
class C {
public:
std::shared_ptr<D> pointer;
~C() {
std::cout << "A was destroyed" <<
std::endl;
}
};
class D {
public:
std::shared_ptr<C> pointer;
~D() {
std::cout << "D was destroyed" <<
std::endl;
}
};
int main() {
std::shared_ptr<C> c = std::make_
shared<C>(); std::shared_ptr<D> d =
std::make_shared<D>(); c->pointer = d;
d->pointer = c;

return 0;
}
```

As a result, neither C nor D will be destroyed. Because the pointer within c, d also refers c, d, c, d's reference count reaches 2, and the scope is exited. The reference count of this region may only be decremented by one when the c, d smart pointer is destroyed. This causes the c, d object's memory area reference count to be non-zero, but the external has no method of finding this region, resulting in a memory leak.

CHAPTER 6

Preprocessing and Compilation

IN THIS CHAPTER

> ➤ Compiling your source code

> ➤ Preprocessor directives in C++

> ➤ Conditionally compiling classes and functions with enable_if

> ➤ Attributes in C++

> ➤ Providing metadata to the compiler with attributes

In the previous chapter, we studied what memory management is and why it's essential, as well as what memory management operators are and why they're helpful. Furthermore, we also learned what dynamic memory

DOI: 10.1201/9781003214762-6   **293**

allocation is, how to allocate memory dynamically and why memory management is essential and what are objects' new and delete operators.

In this chapter, we will focus on compiling our code. Also, we will learn about several types of processors, how to compile our basic source code in Visual Studio, and what preprocessor directives are in this chapter. Furthermore, we discover what enable if is and when it should be used. What are enable if Classes and what are the scenarios that they may be used for? How to use std::enable if and enable if to compile classes and functions on a conditional basis, as well as how to create a member function conditionally. Furthermore, what are attributes in C++, and what is the list of them? What is the difference between standard and non-standard qualities, and how can we tell the difference? Since C++11, the following has changed, as well as the distinctions between C++ and C# features.

The term "compiling source code" refers to the process of converting it into a working program. Object code refers to the machine code that is actually executed by the computer. A compiler converts source code to object code, but the object code isn't yet ready to be turned into a program. A linker is required before object code can be turned into a program.

Aside from learning about pointers and memory management, one of the most difficult aspects of learning C++ was figuring out how to effectively build code while utilizing third-party libraries. As a game developer, we rely on libraries for many parts of our game, such as graphics and physics, and compiling an empty project with these libraries included is difficult.

THREE STEPS PROCESS

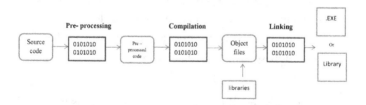

Compiling a C++ program entails turning the source code we've produced (.cpp, .c, .h, .hpp files) into an executable or library that can execute on a certain platform. This procedure may be broken down into three stages:

1. **Preprocessing:** Preprocessor directives in C++ are recognized in code by the prefix # and describe behavior to be performed on source code before it is built. More information on preprocessor directives may be found here. These behaviors are carried performed at the initial stage of building a C++ program utilizing the preprocessor.

   The preprocessor directive determines the specific nature of the pre-actions. Processor's we frequently break code into distinct files, for example, to make it easier to organize and understand. The #include directive is used to link code in one file with code in another. The preprocessor takes this #include and copies and pastes the code from that header file into the file that includes it in our C++ programme. This saves us time and reduces the possibility of errors that manual code copying between files might create.

They include directive is one example of a pre-defined directive; check this page for other instances. All preprocessor directives in our code will have been handled by the compiler's preprocessor by the conclusion of the preprocessor step, and the outputted code is now ready to be built.

2. **Compiling:** The next phase in the process is compiling, which is concerned with converting the source code that we write into machine code that a computer can comprehend.

Compilation in C++ is a two-step procedure. The compiler begins by converting the source code into assembly language. Assembly is a low-level programming language that is more closely related to a CPU's machine instructions. Second, using an assembler, the source code that has now been translated to assembly language is turned back into real machine code. The outcome is a series of files saved in an object file format, which is an intermediate file format.

Important Note: Machine code is made up of binary instructions that are referred to as 'machine language' since the CPU understands them.

For each source code file, an object file with the extensions.obj or .o is produced. All of the machine-level instructions for that file are contained in the object file. It's called an intermediate file since a real executable or library that we can utilize isn't produced until the last stage, linking.

We'll be alerted about any problems in our code that prevent it from compiling during the compilation step. Any problems will be caused by the compiler's inability to comprehend the code we've written. We've effectively screwed up our syntax someplace because the code won't be identifiable as C++. Missing a semi-colon, misspelling a C++ keyword, or adding too many curly brackets to the end of a method are all common compilation errors. If an error is discovered, the compilation process is terminated. We won't be able to build our C++ code until we've repaired all of the problems.

3. **Linking:** The final stage of the process is linking, which involves putting all of the output from the preceding steps together to create the actual executable or library.

   The initial step in this stage is to compile all of the object files into an executable or library. The next step is to link this executable with any external libraries we want to utilize with our program once this has been completed successfully.

   Important Note: A library, such as a math library, is just a reusable collection of functions, classes, and objects with a common purpose.

   Finally, the linker must resolve any dependencies that may exist. This is where any link-related problems will occur. Common problems include not being able to locate a given library or attempting to connect two files that, for example, have the same class name.

   The compiler will provide us with an executable file or library if no problems occur during this stage.

4. **Building:** Another point worth highlighting is that the compilation stages mentioned are combined into a process called build in an IDE like Visual Studio. When building a program, a common approach is to build and then debug.

   What happens is that build generates an executable by compiling and linking the code, or a list of problems, depending on how well we coded since our previous build. Visual Studio will launch the executable file created when we select Start Debugging.

COMPILATION OF A BASIC C++ PROGRAM

We now understand the fundamentals of compiling C++ applications. I thought we might wrap up this post by looking at a simple example to help us remember what we've learned so far.

- **The following are the steps we will take:**

  - Make a folder for our C++ program

  - Go to that folder and open it

  - Using a text editor, we created our C++ application (I used Visual Studio Code

  - Create object files from our source code

  - To make an executable file, we need to link our object files together

- **Make a Location to Save Our C++ Program:** In this stage, we simply use the Windows command md to create a directory with the name HelloWorld at the provided path. We could have created the folder using the file explorer, but this method is much more convenient.

- **Navigate to a Folder:** All we do in this step is use the command cd followed by the location we want to navigate to, in this instance the folder we created in the previous step.

This is something we do to make our lives simpler. If we don't browse to the folder for each file we want to compile, we must provide the complete path name; but, if we are already in the folder, we only need to provide the file name.

Putting together some C++ code

```
class HiWorld
{
public:
    void PrintHiWorld();
};

#include "HiWorld.h"
#include <iostream>
using namespace std;

void HiWorld::PrintHiWorld()
{
    std::cout << "Hi World";
}

#include "HiWorld.h"
```

```
int main()
{
    HiWorld hello;

    hello.PrintHiWorld();

    return 0;
}
```

The main.cpp, HiWorld.h, and HelloWorld.cpp files in the preceding code are all extremely basic programs. Our HelloWorld header file provides a single method PrintHiWorld(), which is implemented in HelloWorld.cpp, with main.cpp handling the actual construction of the HelloWorld object and invoking its function.

- **Compiling:** We just use the cl command followed by all of the.cpp files we want to build to compile and link our application. We may use the command cl/c to compile without linking.

- **Linking:** In order to generate the final executable, we must link our object files in this final stage. To do so, we utilize the LINK command, followed by the newly generated object files.

PREPROCESSOR DIRECTIVES IN C++

Preprocessor Directives

A few lines at the start of nearly every C/C++ program preceded by a hash (#) sign are preprocessor directives. The compiler preprocesses these lines before starting the real compilation. The newline letter "n" signifies the end of these lines; no semicolon ";" is required to complete them.

Preprocessor directives are commonly used to define macros, evaluate conditional statements, include source files, use the pragma directive, regulate line length, and identify errors.

We'll go through some additional preprocessor directives in the sections below:

- Compilation with conditions

- Line control

- Error directive

- **Conditional Compilation:** Conditional compilation directives assist in compiling a specified piece of a program or allow us to forgo compiling a certain part of the program based on certain criteria. We examined two of these directives in our last article: ifdef and endif. We'll talk about #ifndef, #if, #else, and #elif in this post.

  1. **#ifdef:** The simplest conditional directive is #ifdef. A conditional group is the name for this type of block. If the macroname is specified, the controlled text will be included in the preprocessing output. Preprocessing instructions will be included in the controlled text of a conditional. Only if the conditional succeeds are they performed. These can be stacked in several levels, but they must be fully nested. In other words, the closest "#ifdef" (or "#ifndef", or "#if") is always matched by "#endif".

A conditional group can't be started in one file and finished in another.

Syntax:

```
#ifdef MACRO
    controlled text
#endif /* macroname */
```

2. **#ifndef:** We know that if the macroname is defined in the #ifdef directive, the block of statements following it will run properly, but if it is not defined, the compiler will simply skip this block of statements. The #ifndef directive works in the exact opposite way as the #ifdef directive. If the macro or identifier with #ifndef is not defined, the block of statements between #ifndef and #endif will be executed only if the macro or identifier with #ifndef is not declared.

Syntax:

```
ifndef macro_name
    statement1;
    .
    .
    statementN;
endif
```

3. **#if, #else, and #elif:** These directives work together to control the compilation of programme segments based on certain situations. If the condition with the #if directive evaluates to a non-zero value, the group of lines immediately following the #if directive will be executed; if the condition with the #elif

directive evaluates to a non-zero value, the group of lines immediately following the #elif directive will be executed; otherwise, the lines following the #else directive will be executed.

Syntax:

```
#if macro_condition
    statement
#elif macro_condition
    statement
#else
    statement
#endif
```

- **Line control (#line):** When we build a program, there is a risk that it will include an error. When a compiler detects an error in a program, it gives us the filename where the fault was located, as well as a list of lines and the precise line numbers where the error occurred. This makes it simple for us to locate and correct errors.

  The #line directive, on the other hand, allows us to specify what information the compiler should show during compilation problems.

Syntax:

```
#line number "filename"
```

number—the following code line will be allocated this number. From this point on, the line numbers of subsequent lines will be raised one by one.

"filename"—an optional argument that allows us to change the name of the file that will be shown.

- **Error directive (#error):** When this directive is detected in a programme during compilation, it aborts the process and generates an optional error that may be provided as a parameter.

Syntax:

```
#error optional_error
```

optional_error is any error that the user specifies and that will be displayed if this derective is discovered in the application.

WHAT IS ENABLE_IF?

Using boolean conditions to activate SFINAE is simple using std::enable if. It is defined as follows:

```
template <bool Condi, typename res=void>
struct enable_if { };
template <typename res>
struct enable_if<true, res> {
    using type = res;
};
```

That is, enable_if<true, R>::type is an alias for R, but enable_if<false, T>::type is ill-formed since it lacks a type member type.

To limit templates, use std::enable if:

```
int neg(int i) { return -i; }
template <class D>
auto neg(D d) { return -d(); }
```

Because of the ambiguity, a call to neg(1) would fail. However, because the second overload isn't meant to be used with integral types, we may add:

```
int neg(int i) { return -i; }
template <class D, class = typename
std::enable_if<!std::is_
arithmetic<F>::value>::type>
auto neg(D d) { return -d(); }
```

Instantiating negate<int> will result in a replacement failure. The value of std::is arithmetic::value is false. This is not a hard error because of SFINAE; instead, this candidate is simply deleted from the overload list. As a result, neg(1) is limited to only one feasible candidate, which is then called.

When Should We Utilize It?

It's important to remember that std::enable if is only an aid for SFINAE; it's not what makes it function in the first place. Take a look at these two options implementing functionality similar to std:: size, a set size(arg) overload that returns the size of a container or array:

Example:

```
template<typename Cont>
auto size2(Cont const& cont) ->
decltype( cont.size() );

template<typename Elt, std::size_t Size>
std::size_t size2(Elt const(&arr)[Size]);
```

```
// omitted implementation
template<typename Cont>
struct is_sizeable;

template<typename Cont, std::enable_
if_t<std::is_sizeable<Cont>::value,
int> = 1>
auto size3(Cont const& cont);

template<typename Elt, std::size_t Size>
std::size_t size3(Elt const(&arr)
[Size]);
```

These two declarations should be precisely identical in terms of SFINAE, assuming that is sizeable is stated correctly.

enable_if_all/enable_if_any

When a variable template pack is present in the template parameters list, like in the following code snippet:

```
template<typename ...Args> void func(Args
&&...args) { //... };
```

The standard library does not provide a straightforward method to use enable if to apply SFINAE restrictions to all or any of the arguments in Args. The std::conjunction and std::disjunction functions in C++17 fix this problem. Consider the following scenario:

```
// SFINAE constraints all parameters in
args.
template<typename ...Args,
```

```
            std::enable_if_t<std::conjunction_
v<custom_conditions_v<args>...>>* = nullptr>
void func(args &&...args) { //... };

/// SFINAE constraints any parameters in
args.
template<typename ...args,
            std::enable_if_t<std::disjunction_
v<custom_conditions_v<args>...>>* = nullptr>
void func(args &&...args) { //... };
```

If we don't have C++17, there are a couple of workarounds. As shown in the responses to this question, one of these is to utilize a base-case class with partial specializations.

Alternatively, the functionality of std::conjunction and std::disjunction may be implemented by hand in a very straightforward manner. In the example below, I'll show how to combine the implementations with std::enable if to create two aliases: enable if all and enable if any, which perform precisely what they're meant to do semantically.

is_detected

To generalise type trait generation, there are experimental traits detected or, detected t, and is detected that are based on SFINAE.

With the use of template parameters template <typename...>op and typename ... args:

- depending on the validity of Op<args...>, is detected is an alias of std::true type or std::false type.

- **detected t:** alias of Op<args...> or none, depending on Op<args...> validity.

- **detected or:** alias of a struct with value t is detected and type Op<args...> or Default depending on Op<args...> validity, which may be implemented for SFINAE using std::void t as follows:

Example:

```
namespace detail {
    template <class Def, class
AlwVoid,
                template<class...>
class Op, class... args>
    struct detector
    {
        using value_t =
std::false_type;
        using type = Def;
    };

    template <class Def,
template<class...> class Op, class...
args>
    struct detector<Def, std::void_
t<Op<args...>>, Op, args...>
    {
        using value_t =
std::true_type;
        using type = Op<args...>;
    };
}

// indicate detection failure
struct nonesuc {
```

```
        nonesuc() = delete;
        ~nonesuc() = delete;
        nonesuc(nonesuc const&) = delete;
      void operator=(nonesuc const&) =
delete;
    };

template <template<class...> class Op,
class... args>
using is_detected =
        typename detail::detector<nonesuc,
void, Op, args...>::value_t;

template <template<class...> class Op,
class... args>
using detected_t = typename
detail::detector<nonesuc, void, Op,
args...>::type;

template <class Def, template<class...>
class Op, class... args>
using detected_or =
detail::detector<Def, void, Op,
args...>;
```

•

WITH A VAST VARIETY OF CHOICES FOR OVERLOAD RESOLUTION

Enabling just one option through enable_if< > might be inconvenient if we need to choose between multiple choices, because several conditions must be negated as well.

Inheritance, i.e. tag dispatch, can be used to determine the order of overloads.

We test only for what we need, ideally in a decltype in a trailing return, rather than checking for the item that needs to be well-formed and also the negation of all the other versions requirements.

This may result in multiple well-formed options; we distinguish between them by using "tags", which are analogous to iterator-trait tags (random access tag et al). This is because a direct match is preferable to a base class, which in turn is preferable to a base class of a base class, and so on.

Example:

```cpp
#include <algorithm>
#include <iterator>

namespace detail
{
    // infinite types that inherit
from each other
    template<std::size_d N>
    struct pi : pi<N-1> {};
    template<>
    struct pi<0> {};

    // the overload we want to be
preferred have a higher N in pick<N>
    // this is the first helper
template function
    template<typename D>
    auto stable_sort(D& d, pi<2>)
        -> decltype( t.stable_sort(),
void() )
```

```cpp
    {

        t.stable_sort();
    }

    template<typename D>
    auto stable_sort(D& d, pick<1>)
        -> decltype( d.sort(), void() )
    {

        d.sort();
    }

    // this helper will be picked last
    template<typename D>
    auto stable_sort(T& d, pick<0>)
        -> decltype( std::stable_
sort(std::begin(t), std::end(t)),
void() )
    {
        // the container have neither
a member sort, nor member stable_sort
        std::stable_sort(std::begin(d),
std::end(d));
    }

}

// The user invokes this function.
With the aid of "tags", it will route
the call to the appropriate
implementation.template<typename D>
void stable_sort(D& d)
{
```

```
    // Use a N that is greater than
the previous ones. This will select
the highest well-formed overload.
    detail::stable_sort(d,
detail::pick<20>{});
}
```

enable_if Class

For SFINAE overload resolution, conditionally creates an instance of a type. If and only if Condition is true, the nested typedef enable if<Condition,Type>::type exists—and is a synonym for Type.

Syntax:

```
template <bool B, class D = void>
struct enable_if;
```

Parameters:

- **B:** The value that determines if the resultant type exists

- **D:** If B is true, D is the type to instantiate

Remarks:

- Enable if<B, D> contains a nested typedef called "type" that is a synonym for D if B is true

- Enable if<B, D> does not contain a nested typedef called "type" if B is false

Syntax:

```
template <bool B, class D = void>
using enable_if_d = typename
enable_if<B,D>::type;
```

In C++, failure to substitute template parameters is not an error in and of itself, and is referred to as SFINAE (substitution failure is not an error). Typically, enable if is used to cull the overload set—that is, to eliminate candidates from overload resolution—so that one definition can be discarded in favor of another.

- **Here are four scenarios to consider:**

  - **Scenario 1:** Wrapping a function's return type:

  ```
  template <yours_stuff>
  typename enable_if<yours_condition,
  yours_return_type>::type
      yoursfunction(args) {// ...
  }
  // It's more succinct using the
  alias template.
      template <yours_stuff>
  enable_if_t<yours_condition,
  yours_return_type>
  yoursfunction(args) {// ...
  }
  ```

  - **Scenario 2:** Adding a default argument to a function parameter:

  ```
  template <yours_stuff>
  yours_return_type_if_present
      yoursfunction(args, enable_if_
  t<yours condition, FOO> = BAR)
  {// ...
  }
  ```

- **Scenario 3**: Adding a default argument to a template parameter:

```
template <yours_stuff, typename Dummy
= enable_if_t<yours_condition>>
rest_of_function_declaration_goes_
here
```

- **Scenario 4:** We may encapsulate the type of a non-templated parameter in our function:

```
template <typename D>
void your_function(const D& d,
    enable_if_t<is_
something<D>::value, const string&>
s) {// ...
}
```

Because constructors and conversion operators don't have return types, Scenario 1 doesn't work.

Scenario 2 does not mention the parameter. We might say: :type Dummy = BAR, but the name Dummy is meaningless, and giving it one would almost certainly result in a "unreferenced parameter" error. We must select a FOO function parameter type as well as the BAR default argument. We might say int and 0, but users of our code may unintentionally give an additional integer to the method, which would be disregarded. Because practically nothing is convertible to void **, we advocate using void ** and either 0 or nullptr instead:

```
template <yours_stuff>
your_return_type_if_present
```

```
yoursfunction(args, typename enable_
if<yours_condition, void **>::type =
nullptr) {// ...
}
```

Scenario 2 is equally applicable to regular constructors. It does not work for conversion operators, however, because they are unable to accept additional parameters. It also doesn't work for variadic constructors since adding more arguments renders the function parameter pack non-deduced, defeating the goal of enable if.

The name Dummy is used in Scenario 3, but it is not required. If we believe "typename = typename" seems strange, we may use a "dummy" name instead—just don't use one that might be used in the function description. If we don't specify a type for enable if, it will default to void, which is OK because we don't care what Dummy is.

Scenario 4 addresses the wrapping restriction of Scenario 1 by working with constructors without return types. Scenario 4 is, however, restricted to non-templated function parameters, which are not usually accessible. (When Scenario 4 is applied to a templated function parameter, template argument deduction is disabled.)

enable if is a powerful tool, but it may also be hazardous if used incorrectly. Because it's intended to make candidates vanish before overload resolution, when it's utilized incorrectly, the results may be rather perplexing. Here are a few suggestions:

- To choose between implementations at compile time, don't use enable if. Never write two enable ifs, one for CONDITION and the other for !CONDITION.

Use a tag dispatch pattern instead, such as an algorithm that chooses implementations based on the strengths of the iterators they're given.

- To enforce requirements, don't use enable if. Use static assert to check template arguments and, if the validation fails, provide an error rather than picking another implementation.

- When we have an overload set that makes otherwise acceptable code unclear, use enable if. This is most common in implicitly converting constructors.

TO BUILD A MEMBER FUNCTION CONDITIONALLY, USE std::enable_if

SFINAE only works if substituting a template argument in argument deduction results in an ill-formed construct. There is no such thing as a substitute.

I had the same notion and tried using std::is same T, int >::value and! which returns the same value as std::is same T, int >::value.

That's because when the class template is instantiated (which happens, among other things, when we create an object of type Y<int>), it instantiates all of its member declarations (not necessarily their definitions/bodies!). Its member templates are also included. T is known at this point, !std::is same <T, int >::value returns false. As a result, a class called Y<int> will be created.

Example:

```
class B<int> {
    public:
```

```
        /* instantiated from
        template < typename = typename
std::enable_if<
            std::is_same< C, int >::value
>::type >
        C foo() {
            return 10;
        }
        */

        template < typename = typename
std::enable_if< true >::type >
        int fooo();

        /* instantiated from

        template < typename = typename
std::enable_if<
            ! std::is_same< C, int
>::value >::type >
        C fooo() {
            return 10;
        }
        */

        template < typename = typename
std::enable_if< false >::type >
        int fooo();
};
```

Because std::enable if <false>::type refers to a non-existent type, the declaration is invalid. As a result, our software is unusable.

We must make the enable if of the member templates rely on a parameter of the member template itself. Because the entire type is still dependent, the declarations are legitimate. Argument deduction for their template arguments occurs when we try to call one of them, and SFINAE occurs as anticipated.

USING ENABLE_IF TO COMPILE CLASSES AND FUNCTIONS ON A CONDITIONAL BASIS

C++'s template metaprogramming capability allows us to create generic classes and functions that operate with any type. This can be an issue in some cases since the language lacks a method for putting limits on the types that can be used as template arguments. However, we may still accomplish this by employing metaprogramming techniques and exploiting a concept known as substitution failure is not an error, or SFINAE. This recipe will show us how to use type restrictions in templates.

Making Preparations

For many years, developers have utilized the enable if class template in combination with SFINAE to impose restrictions on template types.

The enable if template family is now part of the C++11 standard, and it works like this:

Syntax:

```
template <bool Test, class C = void>
struct enable_if
{ };
template<class C>
```

```
struct enable_if<true, C>
{
typedef C type;
};
```

We must include the <type traits> header in order to utilise std:: enable if.

How Does It Work?

Consider the following examples of how std::enable if may be used in several contexts to achieve different goals:

- To activate a class template only for types that match a given criteria on a class template parameter:

Example:

```
template <typename D,
        typename = typename
std::enable_if<std::is_pod,D>::value,
D>:: type>
class pod_wrap
{
D value;
};
struct point
{
int a;
int b;
};
pod_wrap<int>
pod_wrap<point>
pod_wrap<std::string>
```

- To allow a function template only for types that match a given criteria on a function template parameter, function parameter, or function return type:

Example:

```
template<typename D,
typename = typename std:: enable_if<
std::is_integral<D>:: value, D>::type>
auto mul (D const x, D const y)
{
return x * y;
}
auto k1 = mul(2,3);
auto k2 = mul(1.2,2.4);
```

To reduce the amount of cluttered code we end up writing when we use std: : enable_if, we may use alias templates to define two aliases, EnableIf and DisabledIf:

```
template <typename Test, typename D = void>
using EnableIf = typename std: : enable_
if<! Test : : value, D >:: type;
```

```
template <typename Test, typename D = void>
using DisableIf = typename std: : enable_
if<! Test : : value, D >:: type;
```

The following definitions are identical to the ones shown above based on these alias templates:

```
template <typename D, typename =
EnableIf<std: : is_pod<D>>>
class pod_wrap
```

```
{
D value;
};
template<typename D, typename =
EnableIf<std: : is_integral<D>>>
auto mul(D const x, D const y)
{
return x * y;
}
```

How Does It Work?

The compiler uses the SFINAE rule while doing overload resolution, which is why std::enable_if works. Before we get into how std::enable_if works, it's important to understand what SFINAE is.

When the compiler sees a function call, it must create a list of potential overloads and choose the best match for the call depending on the function call's parameters. The compiler must evaluate function templates as well while constructing this overload set, and must execute a replacement for the given or inferred types into the template parameters.

According to SFINAE, instead of returning an error when the replacement fails, the compiler should simply delete the function template from the overload list and proceed.

Consider the two overloads of the function func () that follow.

The first overload is a function template with a single T::data type parameter, which implies it can only be instantiated with types with a data type inner type.

The second overload is an int-type function with a single argument:

Example:

```
template <typename B>
void func (typename B: : data_type
const d)
{ std: :cout << "func" << std: :endl; }

void func (int const d)
{ std: : cout << "func" std: :endl; }

template <typename D>
struct some_type
{
using data_type = D;
};
```

If a call like func (42) is encountered, the compiler must look for an overload that can take an int argument. Because int does not have a data type member, the output void func (int::data_type const) is incorrect when it creates the overload set and substitutes the template parameter with the supplied template argument. The compiler will not report an error and halt because of SFINAE; instead, it will just disregard the overload and proceed. It then looks for void func (int const), which is the best match it can find.

If the compiler finds a call like func<some type<<int>>(42), it creates an overload set that includes void func(some type<int>: :data_type const> and void func (int const), with the first overload being the best match in this case; no SFINAE is used.

If the compiler finds a call like func ("string"s), it will again rely on SFINAE to disregard the function template, because std: : basic_string does not have a value type member. The overload set, however, does not include any matches for the string parameter this time; as a result, the program is ill-formed, and the compiler issues an error and exits.

There are no members in the class template enable if<bool, D>, but its partial specialization enable if<true, D> does include an inner type named type, which is a synonym for D. The inner member type is available when the compile-time statement given as the first parameter to enable if evaluates to true, otherwise it is not.

When the compiler finds a call like mul (2, 3), it tries to substitute int for the template argument T; because int is an integral type, std: :is_ integral evaluates to true, and a specialization of enable_ if that defines an inner type named type is created. As a result, the EnableIf alias becomes a synonym for this type, which is void (due to the typename D = void expression). The result is an int mul<int, void> (int x, int y) function template that may be invoked with the provided parameters.

When the compiler finds a call like mul (1.2, 2.4), on the other hand, it tries to replace double for the template argument D. Because this isn't an integral type, the std::enable_if condition evaluates to false, and the class template doesn't specify an inner member type. This causes a substitution error, but the compiler, according to SFINAE, will not generate an error and will continue. However, because no alternative overload is discovered, there will be no way to invoke the mul () method. As a result, the program is deemed ill-formed, and the compiler generates an error.

A similar issue arises when using the class template pod wrapper. It contains two template type parameters: the first is the wrapped POD type, and the second is the result of the enable if and are pod substitutions. The inner member type from enable if exists if the type is a POD type (as in pod wrapper) and it replaces the second template type argument. If the inner member type is not a POD type (like in pod wrapper <std: : string>), the substitution fails with a message like "too few template parameters".

ATTRIBUTES IN C++

Attributes are a fundamental element of contemporary C++ that allow the programmer to provide extra information to the compiler in order for the compiler to impose constraints (conditions), optimize certain portions of code, or generate specific code. In basic words, an attribute is a note or annotation to the compiler that gives more information about the code for the sake of optimization and imposing specific constraints on it. They were first introduced in C++11 and have remained one of the greatest aspects of C++, evolving with each subsequent version.

The Purpose of Attributes in C++

- **Is to enforce code constraints:** A constraint is a requirement that the parameters of a function must fulfill in order for it to be executed (precondition).

This was how the code for specifying restrictions was written in prior versions of C++.

Example:

```
int d(int j)
{
  if (j > 0)
    return j;
  else
    return -1;
  // code
}
```

It improves the readability of our code and eliminates the clutter created by the argument checking code placed inside the method.

Example:

```
int d(int j)[[expects:j > 0]]
{
  // code
}
```

- **To provide the compiler with additional information for optimization purposes:** Compilers are quite adept at optimization, yet they still trail below humans in several areas and suggest inefficient generic code. This is due to a shortage of information on the "problem" that humans face. To address this issue, the C++ standard has included several additional characteristics that allow us to tell the compiler a little bit more than just the code statement. The term "probable" is one such example.

Example:

```
int d(int j)
{
  switch (j) {
  case 1:
    [[fallthrough]];
    [[likely]] case 2 : return 1;
  }
  return -1;
}
```

When a statement is preceded by a likely, the compiler does specific optimizations on that statement, improving the code's overall performance.

- **Suppressing specific warnings and faults in the code that the author meant to have:** Rarely, a programmer may purposefully try to produce incorrect code, which will be discovered by the compiler and reported as an error or a warning. An unused variable that has been kept in that state for a specific reason, or a switch statement with the break statements not inserted after some instances to cause fall-through situations, are two examples. C++ has properties like [maybe unused] and [fallthrough] that prevent the compiler from issuing warnings or errors in such situations, allowing to avoid problems and warnings.

Example:

```
#include <iostream>
#include <string>

int main()
{

  // Set debug mode
  [[maybe_unused]] char mg_brk = 'E';

  // this unused variable generates
no warnings or errors from the
compiler.

}
```

The following is a list of standard C++ attributes:

1. **noreturn:** The function does not return a value when noreturn is used.

   Syntax:
   ```
   [[noreturn]] void g();
   ```

   When looking at the code above, the issue of why noreturn is used when the return type is actually void emerges. If a function is of the void type, it returns to the caller without a value, but if the function never returns to the caller (for example, an endless loop), adding a noreturn attribute offers the compiler clues to optimise the code or create better warnings.

Example:

```
#include <iostream>
#include <string>

[[noreturn]] void d()
{
  // There is some code that does not
return anything.
  // return the caller's control
  // The function returns in this
instance
  // without providing a value to the
caller
  // This is why the error "noreturn'
function does return" appears.
}

void h()
{
  std::cout << "Code is intented to
reach";
}

int main()
{
  d();
  h();
}
```

2. **deprecated:** Indicates that the name or entity specified with this property is no longer valid and should
   be avoided for whatever reason. Namespaces, functions, classes, structures, and variables can all have
   this property.

Syntax:

```
[[deprecated("deprecation reason ")]]

// For Struct
struct [[deprecated]] D;

// For Functions
[[deprecated]] void g();

// For namespaces
namespace [[deprecated]] cs{}

// For variables
[[deprecated]] int y;
```

Example:

```
#include <iostream>
#include <string>

[[deprecated("Buffer overflow is a
risk")]] void gets(char* str)
{

  // Code for gets dummy

}

void gets_n(std::string& str)
{
  // Dummy code
  char st[100];
  std::cout << " Executed
Successfully";
```

```
  std::cin.getline(st, 150);
  str = std::string(st);
  // new gets code
}

int main()
{
  char c[150];
  gets(c);

  // std::string str;
  // gets_n(str);
}
```

3. **nodiscard:** The caller should not ignore the return values of entities defined with nodiscard. Simply put, if a function returns a value and is tagged nodiscard, the caller must use the return value rather than trash it.

Syntax:

```
// Functions
[[nodiscard]] void g();

// Struct declaration
struct [[nodiscard]] my_struct{};
```

The primary difference between nodiscard with functions and nodiscard with class declarations is that with functions, nodiscard only applies to the function that is declared no discard, whereas with struct/ class declarations, nodiscard applies to all functions that return the nodiscard marked object by value.

Example:

```cpp
#include <iostream>
#include <string>

// Return value
[[nodiscard]] int g()
{
  return 0;
}

class[[nodiscard]] my_class{};

// Automatically becomes nodiscard
marked
my_class funn()
{
  return my_class();
}

int main()
{
  int z{ 1 };

  // No error as value is utilised
  // z= g();

  // Error : Value is not utilised
  g();

  // Value not utilised error
  // funn() ;
  return z;
}
```

4. **maybe_unused:** Suppresses warnings for any entities that aren't in use (For example: An unused variable or an unused argument to a function).

Syntax:

```
//Variables
[[maybe_used]] bool log_var = true;

//Funcs
[[maybe_unused]] void
log_without_warning();

//Func args
void f([[maybe_unused]] int x, int y);
```

Example:

```
#include <iostream>
#include <string>

int main()
{

  // Set debug mode
  [[maybe_unused]] char mg_brk = 'E';

  // This unused variable generates no
warnings or errors from the compiler.
}
```

5. **fallthrough:** [[fallthrough]] indicates that a switch statement's fallthrough is intended. A programmer's error is generally missing a break or return in a

switch statement, although fallthrough can result in very succinct code in some circumstances, thus it is employed.

Example:

```
void process_alert(Alert alert)
{
  switch (alert) {
  case Alert::Yellow:
    evacuate();
  // Compiler emits a warning here

  case Alert::Red:
    trigger_alarm();

    // this needs semicolon
    [[fallthrough]];
  // Warning suppressed by
[[fallthrough]]

  case Alert::Blue:
    record_alert();
    return;

  case Alert::Orange:
    return;
  }
}
```

6. **likely:** For optimization of assertions that have a higher chance of being executed than others. For testing reasons, Likely is now included in the current version of the GCC compiler.

Example:

```
int g(int j)
{
  switch (j) {
  case 1:
    [[fallthrough]];
    [[likely]] case 2 : return 1;
  }
  return 2;
}
```

7. no_unique_address: Indicates that this data member does not need to have a unique address from the rest of its class's non-static data members. This indicates that if a class has an empty type, the compiler can optimize it via empty base optimization.

Example:

```
struct Empty {
};

struct Y {
  int j;
  Empty e;
};

struct Z {
  int j;
  [[no_unique_address]] Empty d;
};

int main()
{
```

```
// the size of any object of
// empty class type is at least 1
static_assert(sizeof(Empty) >= 1);

// at least one more byte is needed
to give d a unique address
static_assert(sizeof(Y) >=
sizeof(int) + 1);

// empty base optimization
static_assert(sizeof(Z) ==
sizeof(int));
}
```

8. **expects:** It defines the conditions (in the form of a contract) that must be met by the arguments in order for a function to be run.

Syntax:

```
return_type func ( args...) [[expects
: precondition]]
```

There is a distinction between standard and non-standard characteristics

Standard Attributes	Non Standard Attributes
The standard specifies them, and they are present in all compilers.	Vendors of compilers provide this information and they aren't found in all compilers.
Without any warnings or problems, the code is entirely portable.	Despite the fact that code for non-standard attributes in "standard syntax" has become portable (since C++17), compilers still generate warnings and errors.

(Continued)

Standard Attributes	Non Standard Attributes
Attributes are written using the [[atr]] standard syntax.	Some attributes are expressed in a compiler-specific term like declspec() or __attribute__, while others are written in non-standard syntax.
There are no standard characteristics in any namespace that surrounds it.	Standard syntax is used to write nonstandard characteristics. With the namespace [[namespace::attr]] that surrounds them.

SINCE C++11, THE FOLLOWING HAS CHANGED

- **Ignoring unknown attributes:** Since C++17, one of the most significant modifications to the attribute feature in C++ has been the compiler's explanation of unknown attributes. If the compiler didn't recognize an attribute in C++11 or 14, it would throw an error·and prevent the code from being built. To make it function as a workaround, the programmer had to delete the attribute from the code. This posed a significant problem in terms of mobility. None of the vendor-specific characteristics could be utilized apart from the standard attributes since the code would fail. This made it impossible to use this functionality.

  As a result, the standard made it mandatory for all compilers to disregard characteristics that they did not specify. These allowed programmers to freely use vendor-specific characteristics in their code while yet ensuring that it was portable. When undefined attributes are found, most C++17 compilers now disregard them and provide a warning. This helps programmers to be more versatile with their code since they may now provide numerous characteristics for the same action in various vendor namespaces.

Example: //on their respective the attributes will work

    [[msvc::deprecated]][[gnu::deprecated]] char* gets(char* str) compilers

- **Use of attribute namespaces without repetition:** Some of the requirements for using "non-standard" attributes were loosened in C++17. Prefixing namespaces with a following non-standard attribute is one such example. When several attributes were put together in C++11 or 14, each one had to be prefixed with its surrounding namespace, resulting in the code style seen below.

Example: [[gnu::always_inline, gnu::const, gnu::hot, nodiscard]] int g();

When looking at the code above, it appears to be bloated and crowded. As a result, the committee agreed to simplify the scenario when combining numerous attributes. At this time, the programmer is not required to prefix the namespace with following attributes when they are used simultaneously. This results in the code pattern given below, which appears to be tidy and comprehensible.

Example: [[using gnu:const, always_inline]] int g() {return 0;}

- **Multiple attributes for a single piece of code:** In C++, multiple attributes may now be applied to a single piece of code. In such instance, the compiler evaluates each of the characteristics in the order in which they are written. This enables programmers to create code that can include many restrictions.

Example:

```cpp
#include <iostream>

// Compilers do not yet support this
feature, but it will be added in the
future.

[[nodiscard]] int g(int h) [[expects:h
> 0]]
{
  std::cout << " Always greater than 0"
      << " and return val "
      << "always utilized";
}
```

DIFFERENCES BETWEEN C++ AND C# CHARACTERISTICS

There is a significant difference between C# and C++ attributes. Deriving from System in C# allows the programmer to specify additional characteristics. Unlike in C++, where the meta information is fixed by the compiler and cannot be used to define new user-defined characteristics, in C# the meta information is not fixed by the compiler and may be used to define new user-defined attributes. This limitation was put in place to prevent the language from developing into a new form that would have made it more difficult.

ATTRIBUTES IN METADATA

The metadata characteristics describe the content's credentials. These qualifiers can be used to change how the material is processed.

The metadata attributes are commonly used to filter material based on their values. Another common application is to mark content based on its values, for as by highlighting the impacted words in the output. Filtering is often done using audience, platform, product, and otherprops, and flagging is done with the same characteristics plus rev. For example, designating stages in a job as optional or mandatory, status and significance are utilized for tool-specific or transform-specific behavior.

A metadata attribute, in general, offers a list of one or more qualification values separated by whitespace. The audience attribute administrator programmer, for example, classifies the material as being relevant to administrators and programmers.

The audience, platform, and product metadata for a subject can be represented using properties on the topic element or components in the topic prologue. While the metadata components are more descriptive, the values have the same meaning and can be used together.

- **audience:** When the values from the enumerated attributes of the audience metadata element are used in the audience attribute of a content element, they have the same meaning. The "user" value, for example, has the same meaning whether it appears in the type property of a topic's audience element or the audience attribute of a content element. The idea applies to the audience element's type, job, and experience level properties.

The audience attribute's values can also be used to point to a more detailed description of an audience in an audience element. When referring to the same audience in an audience attribute, use the name of the audience from the audience element. The audience property accepts a list of values separated by blanks that may or may not match the name value of any audience components.

- **platform:** The operating system, hardware, or other environment can all be considered platforms. This property is the subject metadata's counterpart of the platform element.

  The platform property accepts a list of values separated by blanks, which may or may not correspond to the content of a platform element in the prologue.

- **product:** The name, version, brand, or internal code or number of the product or component. This property is the subject metadata's counterpart of the prodinfo element.

  The product property accepts a list of values separated by blanks, which may or may not match the prodname element's value.

- **importance:** The importance of the material is measured in terms of its priority. This property accepts a single enumeration value.

- **rev:** The revision level's unique identifier.

- **status:** The current state of the content and this property accepts a single enumeration value.

PROVIDING METADATA TO THE COMPILER WITH ATTRIBUTES

When it comes to features that enable reflection or introspection on types or data, as well as standard procedures for defining language extensions, C++ has been severely lacking. As a result, compilers have created their own extensions specifically for this purpose. The VC++ __declspec() specifier and the GCC __attribute__(...) specifier are two examples. C++11, on the other hand, adds the idea of attributes, which allow compilers to incorporate extensions or even embedded domain-specific languages in a standard fashion. The new C++ standards establish a number of characteristics that all compilers must support.

How To Do It

Use standard attributes to provide hints for the compiler about various design goals:

- **To gurantee that the return value from a function cannot be overlooked, declare the function with [[nodiscard]] attribute:**

```
[[nodiscard]] int get_value( )
{
return 30;
}
get value( );
```

- Alternatively, we may use the [[nodiscard]] property to specify enumerations and classes as the return type of a function; in this case, the return result of any function yielding such a type cannot be ignored:

```
num class [[nodiscard]] Recurncodes {
OK, NoData,  Error };
ReturnCodes get_value4 ()
{
return Returncode ::OK ;
}

sttuct [[nodiscard]] Item { };

Item get_value5()
{
return Item { };
}
get_value4()
get_value5()
```

- Declare functions or types that are considered deprecated with the [[deprecated]] attribute to ensure that the compiler issues a warning when they are used:

```
[ [ deprecated ("Use function2( )" ] ]
void function( )
{
}
Class [ [ deprecated ] ] fooo
{
};
```

- Use the [[may_unused]] attribute to prevent the compiler from emitting a warning for unused variables:

```
double run ( [ [ maybe_unused ] ] int f,
double g)
{
return 2 * g;
}
[ [ maybe_unused ] ] auto c = get_
value ( ) ;
```

- Use the [[fallthrough]] property to prevent the compiler from flagging the deliberate fall-through case labels in a switch statement with a warning:

```
void option2 ( ) {}
void option3 ( ) {}

int alternative = get_value ( );
switch (alternative)
{
case2:
option2 ( );
[ [ fallthrough ] ];
}
{
case3:
option3 ( );
}
```

How Does It Work?

The attributes are a very versatile element of C++; they may be used practically anywhere, but their real usage is determined for each attribute. Types, functions, variables, names, code blocks, and whole translation units can all benefit from them.

Attributes are given using double square brackets (for example, c c attrl] d), and a declaration can have several attributes (for example, [[attrl, attr2 attr3]).

Attributes can have arguments, such as [[mode (greedy) D], and they can also be completely qualified, such as [[sys:: hidden]] or [[using sys: visibility (hidden), debug]].

```
int b [ [ attri1] ],  c [ [ attri2] ] ;
int [ [ attri1] ] b, c ;
int [ [ attri1] ] b,  [ [ attri2] ],  c ;
```

Attributes cannot exist in a namespace declaration; however they can occur anywhere in a namespace as a single line declaration. In this example, whether an attribute applies to the next declaration, the namespace, or the translation unit is unique to each attribute:

```
namespace test
  [debug] ] ;
```

Attributes are frequently disregarded or very briefly addressed in current C++ programming books and tutorials, and this is likely due to the fact that developers cannot really use them.

Attributes are frequently overlooked or very briefly addressed in current C+ programming books and tutorials, and this is likely due to the fact that developers cannot create attributes because this language feature is meant for compiler implementations. It may be possible to define user-provided characteristics in some compilers; one such compiler is GCC, which offers plugins that bring more capabilities to the compiler and may also be used to construct new attributes. The standard does, however, specify a number of characteristics that all compilers must support, and knowing how to use them can help us create better code. Some of these were demonstrated in the preceding section's examples. Different versions of the standard have defined these attributes:

- **In C++11:**

  - A function with the [[noreturn]] property does not return.

  - The [[carries dependency]] property specifies that under release-consume std: : memory order, the dependency chain propagates in and out of the function, allowing the compiler to omit superfluous memory fence operations.

- **In C++14:**

  - The attributes [[deprecated]] and [[deprecated ("reason")]] indicate that the object declared with these attributes is deprecated and should not be utilized. These properties indicate that the entity specified with these attributes is deprecated and should no longer be utilized. Classes, non-static data members, typedefs, functions, enumerations, and template specializations can all benefit from these characteristics. The reason string is a parameter that can be left blank.

- **In C++17:**

  - The [[fall through]] property indicates that a switch statement's fall-through across labels is intended. The attribute must be placed on a separate line before the case label.

  - The [[nodiscard]] property specifies that a function's return value cannot be disregarded.

  - The [[maybe unused]] property indicates that an object could be unused, but the compiler should not issue a warning. Variables, classes, non-static data members, enumerations, enumerators, and typedefs can all have this feature.

That brings us to the end of this chapter. In the next chapter, we will turn our attention to coroutines in C++.

CHAPTER 7

Coroutines and Lazy Generators

IN THIS CHAPTER

➤ The Coroutine Abstraction

➤ Coroutines in C++

➤ Generators

➤ Performance

➤ Asynchronous Programming with Coroutines

In this chapter, we will cover what C++ coroutines are, what constraints they have, how to execute them, and what happens when one starts running. We also discover what Heap allocation and promises are. What is the best way for a coroutine to get its promise object within counter. We'll also go through the co_await(), co_yield, and co_return opera-tors in this section. We also learn what generators are and the many generators and Coroutines and C++ for Effective Async.

WHAT ARE C++ COROUTINES?

Coroutines are functions that may be suspended and resumed while maintaining their state. In C++, function evolution is taken a step further. What I propose in C++20 as a novel concept is pretty ancient. The word coroutine was coined by Melvin Conway. In 1963, he used it in a paper on compiler building. Procedures are a subset of coroutines, according to Donald Knuth. A coroutine is a function that may be suspended and restarted at a later time. Coroutines are stackless in the sense that they return to the caller after suspending execution, and the data needed to resume execution is kept independently from the stack. This enables asynchronous sequential code (for example, to handle non-blocking I/O without explicit call-backs) and methods for lazy-computed endless sequences and other applications.

C++20 adds two new ideas to the execution of C++ func-tions with the new keywords co await and co yield.

It is possible to pause and restart the execution of an expression using the co_await expression. When the co_await expression is used in a function, the call auto getRe-sult = func() does not block if the function's result is not accessible. We have resource-friendly waiting instead of resource-consuming blocking.

It can write a generator function using the co_yield expression. Each time the generator function is called, a new value is returned. A generator function is a type of data stream that may be used to choose values. The data stream is limitless. As a result, we are amid a lazy evaluation.

Coroutines are functions that can call each other but do not share a stack, allowing them to pause execution at any time to enter a different coroutine. C++20 coroutines are implemented in the true spirit of C++ as a lovely tiny nugget buried behind piles of trash that we have to wade through to get to the enjoyable part. We were dissatisfied with the design because other recent language updates had been done more gracefully, but not coroutines.

Coroutines are further complicated because the C++ standard library does not provide the heap of trash required to access coroutines, so we must create our own and then wade through it.

Future and promise are widely used to explain and even specify C++ coroutines, which is something to be aware of. The types std::future and std::promise in the C++ <future> header have nothing to do with these words. Specifically, for a coroutine promise object, std::promise is not an acceptable type.

co_await

Now that that's out of the way, C++20 provides us with a new operator called co await. In general, the formula "co_ await a;" does the following:

- Ensures that the current function, which must be a coroutine, saves all local variables to a heap-allocated object.

- Creates a callable object that, when called, resumes execution of the coroutine at the place where the co_ await statement was evaluated.

- Calls (or rather, jumps to) a method of co_await's target object a, sending the callable object from step 2 to that method.

The procedure in step 3 does not restore control to the coroutine when it returns. The coroutine continues to run if and when the callable from step 2 is invoked. The callable in step 2 is similar to a continuation if we've used a language that supports the call with the current continuation or if we've toyed with the Haskell Cont monad.

If a function's definition accomplishes any of the following, it's a coroutine:

- The co_await operator is used to pause execution until it is restarted.

  Syntax:

```
task< > tcp_echo_server() {
  char data[1045];
  while (true) {
    size_t nu = co_await socket.
async_read_some(buffer(data));
    co_await async_write(socket,
buffer(data, nu));
  }
}
```

- co_yield is a keyword that suspends execution and returns a value.

Syntax:

```
generator<int> iota(int c = 0) {
  while(true)
    co_yield c++;
}
```

- co_return is a keyword that completes execution and returns a value.

Syntax:

```
lazy<int> g() {
  co_return 5;
}
```

Restrictions

Variadic arguments, simple return statements, and place-holder return types are not allowed in coroutines (auto or concept).

Coroutines aren't allowed in constexpr functions, con-structors, destructors, or the primary function.

Execution

- **Each coroutine is linked to the following:**

  - Manipulation of the promise objects from within the coroutine. The coroutine uses this object to submit its result or exception.

  - Manipulation of the coroutine handles from out-side the coroutine. This is a non-owning handle for resuming coroutine execution or destroying the coroutine frame.

- The coroutine state is a heap-allocated (unless the allocation is optimized out) internal object that includes.

  - The object of the promise.

  - The variables (all copied by value).

  - A representation of the current suspension point, so resume knows where to go next and destroy knows what variables were in scope locally.

  - Local variables and temporaries with a lifespan that extends beyond the current suspension point.

- **When a coroutine starts running, it does the following things:**

  - Using the new operator allocates a coroutine state object.

  - To the coroutine state, copy all function parameters: by-value parameters are relocated or copied, whereas by-reference parameters are kept as references (and so may become dangling if the coroutine is resumed after the lifetime of the referred object ends).

  - If the promise type contains a function that accepts all coroutine arguments, it is invoked with post-copy coroutine arguments. The default function is used if none is specified.

  - Calls promise to get return object() returns an object and stores it in a local variable. When the coroutine initially suspends, the outcome of that call will be returned to the caller. Exceptions are thrown up to and, including this stage, returned to the caller rather than stored in the promise.

- co_awaits the outcome of calls promise.initial_ suspend(). Suspend_always for lazily-started coroutines and never suspend for eagerly-started coroutines are the two most used Promise kinds.

- When co await promise.initial suspend() returns, the coroutine's body is executed.

- **When a coroutine reaches a point of suspension:**

  - The caller/resumer receives the previously acquired return object, which is implicitly converted to the coroutine's return type if necessary.

- **The following is what a coroutine does when it reaches the co return statement:**

  calls promise.return_void() for:-

  - co_return;

  - co_return expr if expr is of the type void.

  - dropping off a void-returning coroutine's end. The behavior is unknown if the Promise type does not have a Promise::return void() member method.

  - or calls promise.return value(expr) f or co return expr with a non-void type.

  - removes any variables with automatic storage life-time in the reverse order they were created.

- calls promise.

- co_awaits the outcome of final_suspend().

- **If there is an uncaught exception at the end of the coroutine, it does the following:**

  - The exception is caught, and promise is called.

  - From within the catch-block, call unhandled_exception ().

  - calls promise.

  - final_suspend() and co_awaits the result; resuming a coroutine from this point is undefined behavior.

- **When a coroutine state is destroyed, it performs the following:**

  - The promise object's destructor is called.

  - Calls the function parameter copies' destructors.

  - To release the memory occupied by the coroutine state, call operator delete.

  - Returns control to the caller.

HEAP ALLOCATION

Coroutine state is allocated on the heap using the non-array operator new.

If a class-level replacement is defined in the Promise type, it will be utilized; otherwise, the new global operator will be used.

Those arguments will be provided to operator new if the Promise type provides a placement form of operator new that accepts extra parameters, and they match an argument list where the first argument is the size requested (of type std::size_t) and the rest are the coroutine function arguments (this makes it possible to use leading-allocator-convention for coroutines).

Even if a custom allocator is used, the call to operator new can be optimized away if:

- The coroutine state's lifespan is tightly nested within the caller's lifetime.

- If the size of the coroutine frame is known at the call site, the coroutine state is embedded in the caller's stack frame (if the caller is an ordinary function) or coroutine state is embedded in the caller's stack frame.

Promise

We can add field value_ to this type and transfer values from the coroutine to our main function because we know the coroutine state contains an instance of promise type. How do we obtain access to the promise type? This isn't too difficult in the main function. We may maintain our coroutine handle as a std::coroutine_handle<ReturnObject3::promise_type> instead of converting it to a std::coroutine_handle<>. The promise type& that we require will be returned by the function promise() on this coroutine handle.

How May a Coroutine Acquire Its Promise Object Within Counter?

Remember how the Awaiter object in our first example saved a copy of the coroutine handle for main1? Within the coroutine, we can use a similar approach to retrieve the promise:

co_await on a custom awaiter, which returns the promise object. We don't want our new custom awaiter to suspend the coroutine, unlike our prior type Awaiter. After all, we can't put a legitimate return value inside the promise object until we get our hands on it; thus we won't be returning anything valid from the coroutine until then.

Even though our Awaiter::await_suspend method previously returned void, it is now permitted to return a bool. If await suspend returns are false in that situation, the coroutine is not suspended. In other words, a coroutine isn't truly stopped until await_ready returns false, followed by await_suspend (if type bool instead of void) returning true.

As a result, we create a new awaiter type GetPromise with the property promise_type *p_. Its await suspend function saves the address of the promise object in p_ but returns false instead of suspending the coroutine. We've only encountered co_await expressions of type void so far. We also add an await resume method that returns p_ since we want our co_await to return the address of the promise object this time.

```cpp
template<typename PromiseType>
struct GetPromise {
  PromiseType *p_;
  bool await_ready() { return false; }
  bool await_suspend(std::coroutine_
handle<PromiseType> a) {
    p_ = &a.promise();
    return false;
  }
  PromiseType *await_resume() { return p_; }
};
```

await_suspend can return a coroutine handle in addition to void and bool, in which case the returned handle is instantly restarted. GetPromise::await_suspend might have returned the handle h instead of false to continue the coroutine immediately, but this would likely be less efficient.

Example:

```
struct ReturnObject4 {
  struct promise_type {
    unsigned value_;

    ReturnObject4 get_return_object()
{
      return ReturnObject4 {
        .a_ =
std::coroutine_handle<promise_
type>::from_promise(*this)
      };
    }

    std::suspend_never initial_
suspend() { return {}; }
    std::suspend_never final_suspend()
noexcept { return {}; }
    void unhandled_exception() {}
  };
  std::coroutine_handle<promise_type>
a_;
  operator std::coroutine_
handle<promise_type>() const { return
a_; }
};
```

```
ReturnObject4
Counter4()
{
  auto pp = co_await GetPromise<Return
Object4::promise_type>{};

  for (unsigned c = 0;; ++c) {
    pp->value_ = c;
    co_await std::suspend_always{};
  }
}

void
main4()
{
  std::coroutine_
handle<ReturnObject4::promise_type> a
= counter3();
  ReturnObject4::promise_type &promise
= a.promise();
  for (int c = 0; c < 4; ++c) {
    std::cout << "counter3: " <<
promise.value_ << std::endl;
    a();
  }
  a.destroy();
}
```

It's worth noting that our promise object copies i's value from the coroutine into promise type::value_ before passing it to the main function. We could have made value_an unsigned * and returned a reference to the variable I within counter3 in a somewhat confusing way. Because the coroutine's local variables are stored in the heap's coroutine state object and their memory is preserved between co_await calls until the coroutine handle is destroyed; this is something we can achieve. It would be even handier to put I within the return object; however, there is no graceful method to do so due to the way return objects are built.

Using std::coroutine traits, the compiler determines the Promise type from the coroutine's return type.

Let R and Args… indicate the return type and parameter type list of a coroutine, respectively, and ClassT and/*cv-qual*/(if any) denote the class type to which the coroutine belongs and its cv-qualification, respectively, if it is declared as a non-static member function.

- If the coroutine is not declared as a non-static member function, use std::coroutine_traits<R, Args…>::promise type.

- If the coroutine is declared as a non-static member function that is not rvalue-reference-qualified, use std::coroutine_traits<R, ClassD/*cv-qual*/&, Args…>::promise type.

- If the coroutine is specified as a rvalue-reference-qualified non-static member function, use std::coroutine_traits<R, ClassD/*cv-qual*/&&, Args…>::promise type.

co_await

The unary operation co_await suspends a coroutine and hands control back to the caller. Its operand is an expression whose type either defines operator co_await or can be converted to such a type using the current coroutine's type conversion Promise::await_transform.

co_wait expr

- **To begin, expr is transformed to an awaitable in the following way:**

  - The awaitable is expr, as-is, if expr is created by an initial suspend point, a final suspend point, or a yield expression.

  - Otherwise, the awaitable is promise.await_transform if the current coroutine's Promise type contains the member function await_transform.

  - Otherwise, the awaitable is expr as-is.

- **The awaiter object is then acquired in the following manner:** If the operator co_await overload resolution yields a single best overload, the awaiter results from that call (awaitable).

  - For member overload, use co_await(); for non-member overload, use co_await(static_castAwait able&&>(awaitable)).

  - Otherwise, the awaiter is awaitable as-is if overload resolution finds no operator co await.

  - Otherwise, the program is ill-formed if the overload resolution is unclear.

The awaiter object is a temporary materialized from the expression above if it is a prvalue. If the expression above is a glvalue, the object to which it refers to the awaiter object.

Then awaiter.await_ready() is invoked (a shortcut to avoid the expense of suspension if the result is known to be ready or can be finished synchronously). If the result is false when contextually transformed to bool, then.

The coroutine has been halted (its coroutine state is populated with local variables and current suspension point).

The current coroutine's handle is called Handle, and awaiter.await_suspend(handle) is invoked. The suspended coroutine state is visible via that handle inside that function, and it's up to this function to schedule it to restart on some executor or be destroyed (returning false counts as scheduling).

- Otherwise, control is instantly given to the current coroutine's caller/resumer if await suspend returns void (this coroutine stays suspended).

- The value true restores control to the current coroutine's caller/resumer if await suspend returns bool, whereas the value false resumes it.

- If await suspend delivers a coroutine handle for another coroutine, it is resumed (through a call to handle.resume()).

Finally, awaiter.await_resume() is invoked, and the result is the co_await expr expression's result.

The resume point is immediately before the call to awaiter.await_resume if the coroutine was suspended in the co_await expression and later resumed ().

Example:

```
#include <coroutine>
#include <iostream>
#include <stdexcept>
#include <thread>
```

```cpp
auto switch_to_new_thread(std::jthread&
out) {
  struct await {
    std::jthread* a_out;
    bool await_ready() { return false; }
    void await_suspend(std::coroutine_
handle<> h) {
      std::jthread& out = *a_out;
      if (out.joinable())
        throw std::runtime_
error("Output jthread not empty");
      out = std::jthread([k] {
k.resume(); });

      std::cout << "New thread: " <<
out.get_id() << '\n';
    }
    void await_resume() {}
  };
  return awaitable{&out};
}

struct taskk{
  struct promise_type {
    taskk get_return_object() { return
{}; }
    std::suspend_never initial_
suspend() { return {}; }
    std::suspend_never final_suspend()
noexcept { return {}; }
    void return_void() {}
    void unhandled_exception() {}
  };
};
```

```
taskk resuming_on_new_
thread(std::jthread& out) {
  std::cout << "Coroutine started: "
<< std::this_thread::get_id() << '\n';
  co_await switch_to_new_thread(out);
  // awaiter destroyed
  std::cout << "Coroutine resumed: "
<< std::this_thread::get_id() << '\n';
}

int main() {
  std::jthread out;
  resuming_on_new_thread(out);
}
```

The Coroutine Return Object Is As Follows

The return type of counter was disregarded in the preceding case. The language does, however, limit the sorts of coroutines that can be returned. A coroutine's return type call it R must be an object type with the nested type R::promise_type. 2 R::promise type must include a method R get_return object() that returns an instance of the outer type R, among other things. The coroutine function's return value, in this case counter, is returned by get_return object() (). Many explanations of coroutines refer to the return type R as a future, but for clarity's sake, we'll just call it the return object type.

It would be good to just return the handle from the counter instead of providing a coroutine_handle<>* into the counter (). If we place the coroutine handle within the return object, we can do this. We just require promise type::get_return_object to attach the coroutine handle into the return object because that function computes it. How can we acquire a handle to a coroutine from within get_return_object? Because the coroutine state referenced by a coroutine handle contains an instance of promise_type at a given offset, we may calculate a coroutine handle from the promise object using std::coroutine_handle.

co_yield

Getting a coroutine's promise object is so hard because the C++ authors had one specific use case in mind and planned for that rather than the broader situation. Returning values from coroutines, on the other hand, is a valuable use case. To that purpose, the language includes the co_yield operator.

Yield-expression gives the caller a value and stops the current coroutine: It is a fundamental component of resumable generator functions:

Syntax:

```
co_yield expr
co_yield braced-init-lists
```

equivalent to:

```
co_await promise.yield_value(expression)
```

The phrase "co yield e;" is identical to evaluating "co await p.yield value(e);" if p is the current coroutine's promise object. We can simplify the preceding example by adding a yield value function to the promise type within our return object using co_yeild. We no longer need to go through hoops to get our hands on the promise object because yield value is a method on promise_type. This is how the updated code looks:

Example:

```
struct ReturnObject5 {
  struct promise_type {
    unsigned value_;

    ReturnObject5 get_return_object() {
      return {
.         a_ =
std::coroutine_handle<promise_
type>::from_promise(*this)
      };
    }
    std::suspend_never initial_
suspend() { return {}; }
    std::suspend_never final_suspend()
noexcept { return {}; }
    void unhandled_exception() {}
    std::suspend_always yield_
value(unsigned value) {
      value_ = value;
      return {};
    }
  };

  std::coroutine_handle<promise_type>
h_;
};

ReturnObject5
Counter5()
{
  for (unsigned c = 0;; ++c)
    co_yield c;
}
```

```
void
main5()
{
  auto h = counter5().a_;
  auto &promise = a.promise();
  for (int c = 0; c < 3; ++c) {
    std::cout << "counter5: " <<
promise.value_ << std::endl;
    a();
  }
  a.destroy();
}
```

co_return Operator

After reading the first three integers, our main function simply deleted the coroutine state, resulting in an endless stream of integers. What if our coroutine only wishes to create a certain amount of values before indicating the end of the coroutine?

C++ includes a new co_return operator to mark the end of a coroutine. A coroutine can communicate that it is finished in one of three ways:

- "co return e;" can be used by the coroutine to return a final value e.

- The coroutine can finish without a final value using "co_return;" with no value (or a void expression).

- Like the preceding scenario, the coroutine can allow execution to break off at the end of the function.

The compiler adds a call to p.return value(e) on the promise object p in case 1. The compiler calls p.return_void in cases 2–3. (). We may check if a coroutine is finished by

calling a.done() on its coroutine handle h. (Coroutine_
handle::done() should not be confused with corou-
tine_handle::operator bool) (). The latter verifies that the
coroutine handle has a non-null pointer to coroutine memory, not that execution is complete.)

Here's a new version of the counter in which the counter
function chooses to print only three values, while the main
function simply prints data until the coroutine is finished.
There's one more modification we need to make to prom-
ise_type::final suspend(), but first, let's have a look at the
new code, and then we'll talk about the promise object.

Example:

```
struct ReturnObject6 {
  struct promise_type {
    unsigned value_;

    ~promise_type() {
      std::cout << "promise_type
destroyed" << std::endl;
    }
    ReturnObject6 get_return_object() {
      return {
.          a_ =
std::coroutine_handle<promise_
type>::from_promise(*this)
      };
    }
    std::suspend_never initial_
suspend() { return {}; }
    std::suspend_always final_suspend()
noexcept { return {}; }
    void unhandled_exception() {}
```

```
    std::suspend_always yield_
value(unsigned value) {
        value_ = val;
        return {};
    }
    void return_void() {}
  };

  std::coroutine_handle<promise_type>
h_;
};

ReturnObject6
Counter6()
{
  for (unsigned c = 0; c < 3; ++c)
    co_yield c;
  // falling off end of function =>
promise.return_void();
  // (co_return value; => promise.
return_value(val);)
}

void
main6()
{
  auto a = counter5().a_;
  auto &promise = h.promise();
  while (!a.done())
    std::cout << "counter6: " <<
promise.value_ << std::endl;
    a();
  }
  a.destroy();
}
```

There are few things to remember when it comes to co-return. We didn't have a return_void() function on our promise object in the previous examples. That's OK as long as we didn't use co return. If we use co return but don't have the proper return void or return value method, a compilation error regarding the missing function will occur. The good news is that this is the case. The bad news is that we'll receive undefined behavior if we fall off the end of a function and promise type doesn't have a return void method. We'll go into more detail about this in the editorial that follows, but suffice it to say that undefined behavior is terrible—like use-after-free or array-bounds-overflow terrible. So be cautious not to drop off the end of a coroutine that doesn't have a return_void_function on its promise object!

Another thing to keep regarding co return is that promise_type::return void() and promise type::return value(v) return void; they don't return awaitable objects. This is most likely due to a desire to standardize the processing of return values and exceptions. Nonetheless, the dilemma of what to do at the end of a coroutine remains.

Should the compiler make a final change to the coroutine state and halt the coroutine, code in the main function may access the promise object and make sensible use of the coroutine_handle even after evaluating co_return? Shouldn't returning from a coroutine, such an implicit call to coroutine_handle::destroy(), remove the coroutine state?

The final_suspend function on the promise type answers this question. According to the C++ specification,

the function-body of a coroutine is effectively wrapped in
the following:

Syntax:

```
{
        promise-type promise promise-
constructor-args ;
        try
{
            co_await promise.initial_
suspend() ;
            function-body
        }
catch ( ..... )
{
            if
(!initial-await-resume-called)
                throw ;
            promise.unhandled_
exception() ;
        }
    final-suspend :
        co_await promise.final_suspend() ;
    }
```

We implicitly co await the outcome of promise.final_
suspend() when a coroutine returns. If final_suspend truly
suspends the coroutine, the state of the coroutine will
be changed one last time. It will remain valid, and code
outside the coroutine will be responsible for releasing the
coroutine object by executing the destroy() function on
the coroutine handle. If final_suspend fails to suspend the
coroutine, the coroutine state is deleted automatically.

If we're never going to touch the coroutine state again (perhaps because the coroutine just updated a global variable and/or released a semaphore before co return, and that's all we care about), there's no reason to pay for state saving one last time and worry about manually freeing the coroutine state so that final_suspend() returns std::suspend_never. If we need to access the coroutine handle or promise object after it returns, we'll need to use final_suspend(), which returns std::suspend_always.

WHAT ARE GENERATORS?

Generic Generators

The most helpful way to exceptions is to re-throw them in the main routine that calls the generator if we want to develop a generic generator return object type to enable others to write coroutines. Unhandled_exception() may achieve this by using std::current_exception to get a std::exception_ptr, which then puts in the promise object. The generator utilizes std::rethrow_exception to propagate the exception in the main function when this exception ptr is non-NULL.

Another key issue is that, until now, our coroutines computed the initial value (0) as soon as they were called, before the first co_await, and therefore before the return object was built. There are two reasons why we might wish to wait until after the first coroutine suspension to compute the first value. First, when computing values is time-consuming, it may be preferable to store work if the coroutine is never restarted (perhaps because of an error in a different coroutine). Second, because coroutine handles must be explicitly destroyed, things may become complicated if a coroutine throws an exception before being suspended for the first time.

Example:

```
void
g()
{
  std::vector<std::coroutine_handle<>>
coros =
    { mkCoroutineA(), mkCoroutineB() };
  try {
    for (int c = 0; c < 3; ++c)
      for (auto &c : coros)
        if (!a.done())
          a();
  }
  catch (...) {
    for (auto &c : coros)
      a.destroy();
    throw;
  }
  for (auto &a : coros)
    a.destroy();
}
```

Assume that mkCoroutineA() provides a coroutine handle whereas mkCoroutineB() throws an error before its first co await in the example above. The coroutine generated by mkCoroutineA() will never be deleted in this scenario. We could rearrange the code to encapsulate mkCoroutineB in its try-catch block, but this would rapidly become complex when producing many coroutines.

To solve these concerns, the function promise type::initial suspend () can return std::suspend_always, causing mkCoroutineB to be stopped immediately upon entrance before any code in the coroutine has run. In the sample generator below, we utilize this method. It implies that before returning the first value from our generator, we must restart the coroutine.

So, here's our general-purpose generator. A Generator<D> must be returned by a generator that produces type D. The main function checks if the Generator still has an output value and then uses operator() to get the next value.

Example:

```
template<typename D>
struct Generator {
  struct promise_type;
  using handle_type =
std::coroutine_handle<promise_type>;

  struct promise_type {
    D value_;
    std::exception_ptr exception_;

    Generator get_return_object() {
      return
Generator(handle_type::from_
promise(*this));
    }
    std::suspend_always initial_
suspend() { return {}; }
    std::suspend_always final_suspend()
noexcept { return {}; }
    void unhandled_exception() {
exception_ = std::current_exception(); }
    template<std::convertible_to<D>
From>
```

```cpp
    std::suspend_always yield_
value(From &&from) {
      value_ = std::forward<From>(from);
      return {};
    }
    void return_void() {}
  };

  handle_type a_;

  Generator(handle_type a) : a_(a) {}
  ~Generator() { a_.destroy(); }
  explicit operator bool() {
    fill();
    return !a_.done();
  }
  D operator()() {
    fill();
    full_ = false;
    return std::move(a_.promise().
value_);
  }

private:
  bool full_ = false;

  void fill() {
    if (!full_) {
      a_();
      if (a_.promise().exception_)
        std::rethrow_exception(h_.
promise().exception_);
      full_ = true;
    }
  }
};
```

```
Generator<unsigned>
counter7()
{
  for (unsigned c = 0; c < 4;)
    co_yield c++;
}

void
main7()
{
  auto gen = counter7();
  while (gen)
    std::cout << "counter7: " << gen()
<< std::endl;
}
```

One final item to note is that we now remove the coroutine_hande inside the Generator destructor because we know that the coroutine handle is no longer required once the generator is gone.

Greedy Generator

The software that follows is as simple as possible. The function getNumbers returns all integers from start to finish, which inc has incremented. The beginning must be smaller than the ending, and the increment must be positive.

Example:

```
#include <iostream>
#include <vector>

std::vector<int> getNumb(int begin,
int end, int inc = 2) {
```

```
    std::vector<int> numb;        // (1)
    for (int c = begin; c < end; c +=
inc) {
        numb.push_back(c);
    }

    return numb;

}

int main() {

    std::cout << std::endl;

    const auto numb= getNumb(-10, 11);

    for (auto n: numb) std::cout << n
<< " ";

    std::cout << "\n\n";

    for (auto n: getNumb(0, 101, 5))
std::cout << n << " ";

    std::cout << "\n\n";

}
```

Lazy Generator

Example:

```
#include <iostream>
#include <vector>

generator<int> generatorForNumb(int
begin, int inc = 2) {

  for (int c = begin;; c += inc) {
```

```
        co_yield c;

    }

}

int main() {

    std::cout << std::endl;

    const auto numb=
generatorForNumb(-5);

    for (int c= 1; c <= 30; ++c)
std::cout << numb << " ";

    std::cout << "\n\n";

    for (auto n: generatorForNumb(0,
4)) std::cout << n << " ";

    std::cout << "\n\n";

}
```

std::generator: Ranges Synchronous Coroutine Generator

Example:

```
std::generator<int> fib (int maxi) {
co_yield 0;
auto c = 0, d = 1;

for(auto n : std::views::iota(0, maxi))
{ auto next = c + d;
c = d, d = next; co_yield next;
}

}
```

```
int answer_to_the_universe() { auto
coro = fib(6) ;
return std::accumulate(coro |
std::views::drop(4), 0);
}
```

Motivation

Coroutine support in C++ 20 was quite limited. Synchronous generators are standard for coroutines that would be impossible to implement without the technology described in this work. Writing an efficient and appropriately behaved recursive generator; thus, the standard should provide one.

Design

While the proposed std::generator interface is straightforward, there are a few considerations worth noting.

- **input_view:** The std::generator input view is a non-copyable view that models input_range and spawns move-only iterators. The coroutine frame is a one-of-a-kind resource (even if the coroutine handle is copyable). Unfortunately, certain generators can meet the view restrictions but not the view O(1) destruction requirement:

```
template <typename D>
std::generator<D> all (vector<D>
vec) { for(auto & e : vec) {
co_yield e;
}
}
```

Header

There are several places where the generator class may be placed.

- <coroutine>, but coroutine is a low-level header, and generator is reliant on <type traits> and <iterator> bits.

- <ranges>

- A new <generator>

Value Type Can Be Specified Separately

This proposal allows we to define both the "yielded" type, which is the iterator "reference" type (which isn't needed to be a reference), and the value type that corresponds to it. This enables ranges to support proxy types and wrapped references, such as in the following zip implementation:

```
template<std::ranges::input_range Rng1,
std::ranges::input_range Rng2> generator<
std::tuple<std::ranges::range_reference_
t<Rng1>,
std::ranges::range_reference_t<Rng2>,
std::tuple<std::ranges::range_value_type_
t<Rng1>,
std::ranges::range_value_type_t<Rng2>>>
zip(Rng1 R1, Rng2 R2) {
    auto iti1 = std::ranges::begin(R1);
    auto iti2 = std::ranges::begin(R2);
    auto endi1 = std::ranges::end(R1);
    auto endi2 = std::ranges::end(R2); while
(it1 != endi1 && it2 != endi2) {
```

```
co_yield {*iti1, *iti2};
++iti1; ++iti2;
}
}
```

The use of string as a value type in the second example guarantees that the calling code may take the necessary precautions to ensure that iterating over a generator does not invalidate any returned values.

```
// Yielding string literals
  std::generator<std::string_view> string_
views() {
co_yield "foo";
co_yield "bar";
}

std::generator<std::string_view,
std::string> strings() {
co_yield "start";
std::string st;
for (auto stv : string_views()) { st = stv;
st.push_back('!'); co_yield st;
}
co_yield "end";
}
iteration! auto v =
std::to<vector>(strings());
```

Recursive Generator

A "recursive generator" is a coroutine that allows to directly co_yield a generator of the same type to emit its elements as elements of the current generator.

A generator, for example, can co_yield other generators of the same type.

```
generator<const std::string&> delete_
rows(std::string table1, std::vector<int>
ids) {
        for (int Id : ids) {
        co_yield std::format("DELETE FROM
{0} WHERE id = {3}", table1, Id);
    }
}

generator<const std::string&> all_queries() {
    co_yield elements_of(delete_
rows("user", {3, 4, 7 11}));
    co_yield elements_of(delete_
rows("order", {10, 16}));
}
```

Example:

```
Recursive usage of a generator is also
possible.
struct Trees {
Trees* left; Trees* right; int val;
};

generator<int> visit(Trees& trees) {
if (trees.left) co_yield elements_
of(visit(*trees.left)); co_yield trees.
value;
if (trees.right) co_yield elements_
of(visit(*trees.right));
}
```

The ability to directly yield a nested generator provides certain performance advantages versus iterating through the contents of the nested generator and manually yielding each of its elements, in addition to being more succinct.

When using a nested generator, the top-level coroutine's consumer can directly resume the current leaf generator when incrementing the iterator, but manually iterating over elements of the child generator takes O(depth) coroutine resumptions/suspensions each element of the sequence.

Example: The non-recursive version has O(depth) resumptions/suspensions per element and is hence more difficult to write

```
generator<int> slow_visit(Trees& trees) {
if (trees.left) {
for (int y : elements_of(visit(*tree.
left))) co_yield y;
}
co_yield trees.value; if (trees.right) {
for (int y : elements_of(visit(*trees.
right)))

co_yield y;
}
}
```

Exceptions propagated from the body of nested generator coroutines are rethrown into the parent coroutine from the co yield expression instead of propagating from the top-level "iterator::operator++()". This is based on the mental model that "co_yield someGenerator" is semantically identical to manually iterate through the elements and yielding each one.

For example, nested ints() and manual ints() are semantically similar

```
generator<int> might_throw() {
co_yield 0;
throw some_error{};
}

generator<int> nested_ints() {
try
{
co_yield elements_of(might_throw());
} catch (const some_error&) {}
co_yield 1;
}

// nested_ints() is semantically
equivalent
generator<int> manual_ints() {
try {
for (int y : might_throw()) { co_yield y;
}
} catch (const some_error&) {} co_yield 1;
}

void consumer() {
for (int y : nested_ints()) {
std::cout << y << " ";
}

for (int y : manual_ints()) {
std::cout << y << " ";
}
}
```

elements_of

When a nested generator type is convertible to the value type of the current generator, elements_of is a utility function that prevents ambiguity.

Example:

```
generator<int> g()
{
co_yield 22;

}

generator<any> h()
{
co_yield g();
}
```

- **To avoid this issue:**

  - co_yield expression> should always yield the value directly to prevent this problem.

  - co_yield elements of(expression>) return the nested generator's values.

We also suggest that co yield elements of(x) be expanded for convenience to yielding the values of arbitrary ranges other than generators.

```
generator<int> g()
{
std::vector<int> y = /*... */;
co_yield elements_of(y);
}
```

SYMMETRIC TRANSFER

With the symmetric transfer, the recursive form may be accomplished quickly. This functionality was previously provided in a separate recursive_generator type in [CppCoro].

However, owing to HALO improvements and symmetric transfer, it looks that a single type is quite efficient. That functionality comes at a memory cost of three additional pointers per generator. Given the current state of compiler support for coroutines, estimating the runtime cost of our approach is challenging. Our testing, however, reveals no discernible difference between a generator and a recursive_generator, sometimes known as non_recursively. It's worth mentioning that the suggested approach ensures the possibility of HALO optimizations.

While we believe that a single generator type is adequate and provides a superior API, there are three alternatives:

- Support for recursive calls in a single generator type (this proposal).

- A recursive generator type that may return values from either a recursive generator or a generator. That might result in minimal performance gains while using the same amount of RAM.

- A recursive generator type that can only return values from other recursive_- generator types.

The following would be ill-formed if we choose the third option:

```
generator<int> g();
recursive_generator<int> h() {
co_yield g(); // incompatible types
}
```

Instead, we'd have to write:

```
recursive_generator<int> h()
{
for (int y : g()) co_yield y;
}
```

Due to this constraint, deciding whether to return a generator or recursive_generator while constructing a generator coroutine can be tricky since we may not know whether or not this specific generator would be utilized within recursive_-generator at the moment.

Suppose we pick the generator return-type and subsequently wish to yield its elements from a recursive_generator. In that case, we must either manually yield each element one at a time or use a helper function that converts the generator to a recursive_generator. When compared to the situation where the generator was initially built to yield a recursive_generator, both of these choices add runtime cost since they need two coroutine resumptions for each element instead of a single coroutine resumption.

We do not advocate this method because of these drawbacks.

The symmetric transfer is allowed for various generator types as long as the reference type is the same, i.e., the symmetric transfer is not prevented by a different value type or allocator type.

What Is the Best Way to Store the Delivered Value in a Promise Type?

Because the given expression is assured to be alive until the coroutine restarts, storing its address is sufficient. This makes a big yielding type generator efficient. However, due to the extra indirection, it may be pessimistic in terms of producing values smaller than a pointer (The cost of this indirection is unknown, as none of these accesses should cause cache misses.)

Conversions in yielding expressions are avoided as a result of this:

```
generator<string_view> g()
{
co_yield std::string(); // error
}
```

At the cost of extra storage, storing a copy would allow less indirection and the flexibility to yield any values convertible to the yielded type. A generator<const D&> can be utilized to avoid the storage expense.

Support for Allocators

By templating both the generator and the promise_type's new operator on the allocator type, std::generator can handle both stateless and stateful allocators and strives to reduce the interface verbosity for stateless allocators.

Example:

```
std::generator<int, int,
std::allocator<std::byte>>
stateless_examples()
{
co_yield 35;
}
```

```
template <typename Allocator>
std::generator<int, int, Allocator>
allocator_example(std::allocator_arg_t,
Allocator&& alloc)
{
co_yield 35;
}

my_allocator<std::byte> alloc;
input_range auto rng = allocator_
examples<my_allocators<std::byte>>(std
::allocator_arg, alloc);
```

Supporting allocators necessitates keeping a function pointer adjacent to the coroutine frame (to monitor a deallocation function) and, in the case of stateful allocators, the allocator itself.

If an allocator is given, it must be the second argument to the coroutine function, immediately before an instance of std::allocator_arg_t, according to the suggested interface. This method is required to distinguish between the allocator that will be used to create the coroutine frame and the allocators that will be used in the body of the coroutine function.

We believe all standard and user coroutine kinds must have equivalent allocator support interfaces. In reality, the allocator support implementation may be shared between the generator, lazy, and other standard types.

Is It Possible to Postpone Adding Allocator Support for Later?

It's possible that allocator support will be introduced to std::generator in the future. However, because the allocator is a template parameter in the proposed architecture, introducing allocator after std::generator ships would be an ABI break. We urge that we add allocator support immediately, as recommended in this article, and ensure that the architecture remains consistent throughout this cycle's work on std::lazy.

EXPERIENCE AND IMPLEMENTATION

As part of cppcoro and folly, a generator has been given. Cppcoro, on the other hand, provides a distinct recursive generator type, which differs from the suggested architecture.

Folly employs a single recursive generator type that does not support symmetric transfer. Regardless, Folly users found Folly:::Generator to be significantly more efficient than the eager algorithm it replaced.

Ranges-v3 also includes a generator type that is never recursive and precedes the work on move-only views and iterators, which causes the coroutine handler to be ref-counted.

PERFORMANCE AND BENCHMARKS

Because implementations are still being fine-tuned, and performance is highly dependent on whether HALO optimization happens, it is impossible to make conclusive comments regarding the proposed design's performance at this time.

Clang can inline non-nested coroutines whether the implementation supports nested coroutines or not at the time of authoring, but GCC never does HALO optimization.

Support for recursion has no noticeable influence on performance when the coroutine is not inlined.

COMPILING CODE WITH COROUTINES

Because C++20 isn't currently widely supported, we'll need to make sure compiler supports coroutines to use them. We are using GCC 10.2, which appears to allow coroutines if we use the following options while compiling:

```
g++ -fcoroutines -std=c++20
```

HANDLES FOR COROUTINES

The new co_await operator, as previously noted, guarantees that a function's current state is packaged up someplace on the heap and generates a callable object whose activation continues the current function's execution. std::coroutine handle> is the type of the callable object.

A coroutine handle works similarly to a C pointer. It's simple to copy, but it lacks a destructor to release the memory associated with coroutine state. To minimize memory leaks, we should always call the coroutine handle::destroy function to delete coroutine state (though in certain cases a coroutine can destroy itself on completion). When a coroutine handle is destroyed, coroutine handles referencing the same coroutine will lead to the trash and have undefined behavior when executed, just like a C pointer. On the other hand, a coroutine handle remains valid for the duration of a coroutine's execution, even if control passes in and out of the coroutine several times.

COROUTINES AND C++ FOR EFFECTIVE ASYNC

In the same way, everything else in the Windows Runtime focuses on allowing components to provide async methods and making it simple for applications to use those async methods, the Windows Runtime has a fundamental async model. It doesn't provide a concurrency runtime or even any building blocks for creating or consuming async methods on its own. Instead, unique language projections are responsible for all of this.

This is how it should be, and it's not intended to make the Windows Runtime async pattern any easier. Implementing this pattern correctly is no easy task. Of course, this implies that the developer's preferred programming language significantly impacts a developer's view of async in the Windows Runtime. For example, a developer who has only worked with C++/CX could incorrectly but sensibly believe that async is a disaster.

The ideal concurrency framework for a C# developer will be different from the ideal concurrency library for a C++ developer. The language's role, and libraries' role in C++, is to handle the async pattern's mechanics and offer a logical bridge to a language-specific implementation.

In C++, coroutines are the ideal abstraction for both implementing and invoking async functions, but first, let's review how the async model works. Consider the following example of a class with a single static method:

```
struct Sampless
{
  Sampless() = delete;
  static Windows::Foundation::IAsyncAction
CopyAsync();
};
```

By convention, async methods finish in "Async", so we might think of this as the Copy async method. There's a chance there's a blocking or synchronous alternative named Copy. A caller could desire a blocking Copy function for a background thread and a non-blocking, or asynchronous, Copy method for a UI thread that can't afford to block for fear of looking unresponsive.

At first, glance, calling the CopyAsync function appears to be fairly easy. The following C++ code might be written:

```
IAsyncAction async = Sampless::CopyAsync();
```

Even though running the CopyAsync function in a typical procedural fashion, the resultant IAsyncAction isn't the final result of the async method. IAsyncAction is the object that a caller can use to synchronously or asynchronously wait for a result, depending on the context. There are three more well-known interfaces that follow a similar pattern and provide various capabilities for the callee to convey information back to the caller, in addition to IAsyncAction. The four async interfaces are compared in the table.

Name	Result	Progress
IAsyncAction	N	N
IAsyncActionWithProgress	N	Y
IAsyncOperation	Y	N
IAsyncOperationWithProgress	Y	Y

- **Async Interfaces are compared**

- **Expressed Async Interfaces**

```
namespace Window::Foundation
{
  struct IAsyncAction;
  template <typename Prog>
```

```
struct IAsyncActionWithProgress;
template <typename Result>
struct IAsyncOperation;
template <typename Res, typename Prog>
struct IAsyncOperationWithProgress;
}
```

Although IAsyncAction and IAsyncActionWithProgress can wait for an async function to complete, these interfaces do not provide any observable result or return value. IAsyncOperation and IAsyncOperationWithProgress expect the Result type parameter to specify the kind of result that may be expected after the async procedure completes successfully. Finally, the Progress type argument is used by IAsyncActionWithProgress and IAsyncOperationWithProgress to provide the type of progress information anticipated regularly for long-running operations until the async function completes.

There are a few ways to wait for an async method's result. We won't go into detail about each one because it would make this a very long essay. While there are other approaches to async completion, we only advocate async. get method, which does a blocking wait, and the co await async expression, which conducts a cooperative wait in the context of a coroutine. Neither is superior to the other; they just fulfill distinct functions. Let's have a look at how to do a blocking wait.

The get method may be used to create a blocking wait like follows:

```
IAsyncAction async = Sampless::CopyAsync();
async.get();
```

Holding on to the async object has minimal benefit, thus the following form is preferred:

```
Samples::CopyAsync().get();
```

It's crucial to remember that the get method will block the caller thread until the async function completes. As a result, using the get method on a UI thread is not recommended since it may cause the program to become sluggish. If we try to do so in an unoptimized build, an assertion will fire. The get method is excellent for console apps or background threads if we don't want to utilize a coroutine for whatever reason.

The get function will return any result to the caller after the async procedure has been completed. The return type for IAsyncAction and IAsyncActionWithProgress is void. That could be beneficial for an async method that begins a file-copy operation but not so much for an async method that reads a file's contents.

To the example, let's add another async method:

```
struct Sampless
{
  Sampless() = delete;
  static Windows::Foundation::IAsyncAction
CopyAsync();
  static Windows::Foundation::IAsyncOperat
ion<hstring> ReadAsync();
};
```

When using ReadAsync, the get method will send the hstring result to the caller as soon as the process is finished:

```
Sampless::CopyAsync().get();
hstring result = Sampless::ReadAsync().get();
```

If the get method returns true, the resultant string will include the value returned by the async function once it completes successfully. If an error occurs, for example, execution may not return.

The get method is restricted in that it cannot be called from a UI thread, and it does not fully leverage the machine's parallelism because it locks the caller thread until the async function completes. Using a coroutine allows the async function to finish without tying up a valuable resource for an indefinite time.

MEETING THE NEEDS OF ASYNC COMPLETION

Let's take a closer look at how async interfaces operate now that we understand how they work in general. What additional choices do we have if we're not pleased with the blocking delay given by the get method? We'll soon shift gears and focus solely on coroutines, but first, let's look at those async interfaces to see what they have to offer. The contract and state machines indicated by those interfaces are used by both the coroutine support and the get method we saw before.

We won't go into too much detail because we don't need to know much about them, but let's go over the essentials, so we're prepared if we ever have to use them for something unusual. The IAsyncInfo interface is the logical ancestor of all four async interfaces. We can't do much with IAsyncInfo, and, unfortunately, it exists at all because it adds some overhead.

The only IAsyncInfo elements worth considering are Status and Cancel, which can be used to request cancellation of a long-running operation whose result is no longer required.

If we need to know whether an async method has been completed without waiting for it, the Status member can help.

Example:

```
auto async = ReadAsync();
if (async.Status() ==
AsyncStatus::Completed)
{
  auto res = async.GetResults();
  printf("%ls\n", result.r_str());
}
```

Individual versions of the GetResults method are provided by each of the four async interfaces, not by IAsyncInfo itself. They should be called only after the async function has been completed. This is not to be confused with the C++/WinRT get method. Get is implemented by C++/WinRT, whereas GetResults is implemented via the async method. If the async method is still running, GetResults will not block, and if called prematurely, it will most likely produce hresult illegal method call exception. Without a doubt, we can begin to comprehend how the blocked obtain method works. In terms of concept, it looks like this:

```
auto get() cons
{
  if (Status() != AsyncStatus::Completed)
  {
    // Wait for the completion
  }
  return GetResults();
}
```

The actual implementation is a little more complex, but this gives us a good idea of what's going on. The issue is that GetResults is called regardless of whether it's an IAsyncOperation or an IAsyncAction that doesn't return a result. The reason for this is because GetResults is in charge of propagating any errors that may have happened during the async method's implementation and will rethrow an exception if necessary.

The concern remains as to how the caller will wait for the process to be completed. To demonstrate what's involved, we'll create a non-member get to function. We'll begin with the following basic outline, which is based on the preceding conceptual obtain method:

```
template <typename D>
auto get(D const& async)
{
  if (async.Status() !=
AsyncStatus::Completed)
  {
    // Wait for the completion
  }
  return async.GetResults();
}
```

We'll use the return statement unilaterally since our function template will work with all four async interfaces. The C++ language makes special provisions for genericity, which we can appreciate.

Each of the four async interfaces has a unique Completed member that may be used to register a delegate, which will be invoked when the async method completes. In most situations, C++/WinRT will construct the delegate for automatically. All we have to do now is supply a function-like handler, which is generally a lambda:

```
async.Completed([](auto&& async,
AsyncStatus status)
{
  // Done
});
```

The first parameter of the delegate will be the type of the async interface that just finished; however, completion should be treated as a simple signal. To put it another way, don't jam a lot of code inside the Completed handler. We should think of it as a noexcept handler because the async method won't know what to do if something goes wrong inside this handler. So, what are our options?

We could just use an event to inform a waiting thread.

```
template <typename D>
auto get(D const& async)
{
  if (async.Status() !=
AsyncStatus::Completed)
  {
    handle signals = CreateEvent(nullptr,
true, false, nullptr);
    async.Completed([&](auto&&, auto&&)
    {
      SetEvent(signal.get());
    });
    WaitForSingleObject(signal.get(),
INFINITE);
  }
  return async.GetResults();
}
```

Because it's somewhat more efficient, C++/WinRT's get methods utilize a condition variable with a thin reader/ writer lock.

```
template <typename D>
auto get(D const& async)
{
  if (async.Status() !=
AsyncStatus::Completed)
  {
    slim_mutex b;
    slim_condition_variable cd;
    bool completed = false;
    async.Completed([&](auto&&, auto&&)
    {
      {
        slim_lock_guard const guard(b);
        completed = true;
      }
      cd.notify_one();
    });
    slim_lock_guard guard(b);
    cd.wait(b, [&] { return completed; });
  }
  return async.GetResults();
}
```

If we want, we may utilize the mutex and condition variable from the C++ standard library. The idea is that the Completed handler is used to wire up async completion and may be done in various ways.

Naturally, we don't need to build get function, and coroutines are likely to be more accessible and more adaptable in general. Still, we hope this helps us understand some of Windows Runtime's strengths and versatility.

HOW TO MAKE THEM ASYNC OBJECTS

Let's move on to developing or producing implementations of those four async interfaces now that we've looked at the async interfaces and basic completion techniques in general. Implementing WinRT interfaces using C++/WinRT is quite straightforward, as we've previously shown.

```
Implementing IAsyncAction:
struct MyAsync: implement<MyAsync,
IAsyncAction, IAsyncInfo>
{
  // IAsyncInfo member
  Uint42_t Id() cons;
  AsyncStatus Status() cons;
  HRESULT ErrorCode() cons;
  void Cancel() cons;
  void Close() cons;
  // IAsyncAction member
  void Completed(AsyncActionCompletedHand
ler const& handler) cons;
  AsyncActionCompletedHandler Completed()
cons;
  void GetResults() cons;
};
```

The problem arises when we examine how we may put those approaches into practice. While some implementation is not difficult to conceive, doing so effectively requires first reverse-engineering how existing language projections implement them. As we can see, the WinRT async design only works if everyone uses the same state machine and implements these APIs in the same way. Each language projection has the same assumptions about how this state machine is implemented, and awful things will happen if we build it slightly differently.

Thankfully, we don't have to worry about this since, except for C++/CX, each language projection already does it for us. Thanks to C++/WinRT's coroutine functionality, here's a complete implementation of IAsyncAction:

```
IAsyncAction CopyAsync()
{
  co_return;
}
```

This isn't a particularly fascinating implementation, but it is incredibly informative and shows how much C++/WinRT can help us. We can put part of what we've learned so far to the test because this is a complete implementation. A coroutine is a function like CopyAsync. The return type of the coroutine is utilized to stitch together an implementation of both IAsyncAction and IAsyncInfo, which is then brought to life by the C++ compiler at exactly the right time. We'll go over some of those specifics later, but for now, let's have a look at how this coroutine operates. Take a look at the following console app:

```
IAsyncAction CopyAsync()
{
  co_return;
}
int mainfun()
```

```
{
  IAsyncAction async = CopyAsync();
  async.get();
}
```

The CopyAsync method, which returns an IasyncAction, is called by the main function. If we forget what the CopyAsync function looks like in the body or definition, it should be evident that it's just a function that returns an IAsyncAction object.

A co_return or co_await statement is required in a coroutine. It can contain several such statements, but it must have at least one of them considered a coroutine. A co_return statement does not cause any suspension or asynchrony, as one might anticipate. As a result, the CopyAsync method returns an IAsyncAction that completes synchronously or instantly. As an example, consider the following:

```
IAsyncAction Async()
{
  co_return;
}
int mainfun()
{
  IAsyncAction async = Async();
  assert(async.Status() ==
AsyncStatus::Completed);
}
```

The claim is certain to be correct. There is no competition here. Because CopyAsync is merely a function, the caller is stopped until it returns, and the co_return statement is the first opportunity for it to return. This implies that if we have an async contract to implement but don't need to introduce any asynchrony, we may just return the data without blocking or causing a context switch.

Consider the following method, which downloads a value and then returns it cached:

```
hstring m_cache;
IAsyncOperation<hstring> ReadAsync()
{
  if (m_cache.empty())
  {
    // cache value and download
  }
  co_return m_cache;
}
int mainfunc()
{
  hstring mesg = ReadAsync().get();
  printf("%ls\n", mesg.c_str());
}
```

The cache is likely to empty the first time ReadAsync is used, and the result is downloaded. While this is going on, the coroutine will most likely be suspended. Suspension means that control is returned to the caller. The caller is given an async object that has not yet been completed, necessitating the need to wait for completion somehow.

The benefit of coroutines is that they provide a single abstraction for generating async objects and consuming them. An async function may be implemented by an API or component author, but an API consumer or app developer could call it and wait for it to complete using coroutines.

Let's modify the main function from the above code so that a coroutine handles the waiting:

```
IAsyncAction MainAsync()
{
  hstring res = co_await ReadAsync();
  printf("%ls\n", res.c_str());
}
int main()
{
  MainAsync().get();
}
```

The body of the previous main function has been relocated to the MainAsync coroutine. The get method is used in the main function to keep the app from exiting while the coroutine completes asynchronously. The co await statement has been added to the MainAsync function. Rather than blocking the caller thread until ReadAsync finishes, the co await statement is used to wait for the ReadAsync function to finish in a cooperative or non-blocking way. This is what we meant when we talked about a suspension point. The co represents a suspension point await statement.

That brings us to the end of this chapter. So far, in this book, we have covered a lot of topics, such as C++ syntax, data types, functions, compilation, and a lot more! We hope it has been a fruitful coding journey for you.

Appraisal

If speed and productivity are important to you, C++ is an excellent programming language to learn. Due to characteristics such as the pointer, it is the dominant language for Unix systems, allowing developers to build code that they can manage. These are some of the reasons why you should learn this programming language: C++ is a flexible language. It can communicate with practically any other programming language, and it can execute and build programs on almost any machine. It provides excellent performance and quickness. C++ is a programming language that combines high- and low-level capabilities, with the MongoDB database being developed in this language. This language is popular among developers because it gives them complete control over their code. Multiple inheritance, templates, operator overloading, preprocessor instructions, and other features a developer may want are all available in C++. 75 percent of programmers throughout the globe believe C++ to be the greatest choice for competitive programming since it is generally quicker than Java and Python and has the most resources.

DOI: 10.1201/9781003214762-8

Employers want the following qualities in a C++ developer:

C++ is regarded as one of the most difficult programming languages to master. As a result, when recruiting C++ engineers, ensure sure they can do the following:

- Should have prior C++ programming expertise.

- Should be familiar with operating systems such as Unix and Linux.

- Databases, SQL, and NoSQL databases like MongoDB are all important concepts to grasp.

- JavaScript and XML knowledge are required.

- Agile software development technique should be familiar.

The finest languages for competitive programming are C++ and Java. C/C++ is used by the majority of competitive programmers. Java is the second most popular competitive programming language. Because of the Standard Template Library (STL) and Java libraries in each language, C++ and Java are the recommended languages. A knowledgeable coder may build a program that is faster and more powerful than one built in another programming language because of the control C++ offers the user over system resources. As a result, C++ is the preferred language for creating game engines, games, and other resource-intensive applications.

C++ is a flexible language. C++ is a coding language that supports several paradigms. This implies that, in addition to object-oriented programming, it also allows procedural programming. These paradigms are basically various approaches to approaching and solving a coding challenge; two C++ coders might approach and solve the same coding problem in different ways. To achieve the best results, several paradigms might be blended.

Different approaches to problem solving make C++ more difficult, but it also makes it more powerful. There's always something new to learn.

C++ is a performance-oriented language. Despite the fact that C++ is utilized in a wide range of sectors and can be used to develop practically anything, it shines at delivering performance and effectively utilizing system resources. A knowledgeable coder may build a program that is faster and more powerful than one built in another programming language because to the control C++ offers the user over system resources. As a result, C++ is the preferred language for creating game engines, games, and other resource-intensive applications. The majority of AAA games are developed in C++ because they push the limits of current hardware, therefore resource efficiency is critical. This makes C++ the language of choice for some financial applications, where tiny changes in performance in high-frequency trading platforms can be the difference between profit and loss.

C++ is a time-consuming language to learn, but it pays off in the long run. C++ is frequently perceived as being "harder" to learn than other languages due to its complexity. It certainly requires more time and effort to learn than some other languages, but it isn't that difficult. If you need to learn any of the other C-family languages, the time you put in now will pay off later since you will have already completed a substantial portion of the job.

In exchange for your investment, you will have access to a wide selection of career possibilities in a variety of sectors. C++'s long-standing popularity is reflected in the high number of job openings. Not only are many new applications written in C++, but the large numbers of existing systems that use the language need the hiring of coders to maintain them current and updated.

Furthermore, because C++ applications require a huge amount of code to scale, some organizations demand quite big development teams (relative to other languages). As a result, skilled C++ programmers will always be in demand. Finally, many coders are likely to learn C++ because of the fascinating array of career prospects in sectors such as game development. These are difficult areas to enter into, requiring a lot of devotion and hard work.

Job openings in C++: According to the Developer Survey, C++ is the sixth most popular programming language overall, with 19.4% of those polled saying they use it. Other C languages are also popular (which any C++ developer will have a good start on learning). C# (a Microsoft language based on C++ that seeks to integrate the best of Visual Basic) is fourth with 30.9% total use, and C++'s predecessor is seventh with 15.5%.

Gooroo, a skills analytics platform, records around 5,900 C++ jobs posted every month in the United States (approximately 10,000 globally), with an average pay of more than £100,000 in the United States (just over $80,000 globally). Based on experience, an average C++ salary PayScale also has an interesting graph that illustrates how programmer wages and experience are related. In most situations (take, for example, the average.NET developer pay), the increase is steady and predictable. The greater the income, the more years of experience you have. When it comes to C++ developer wages, things are a little more complicated. Salary for entry-level and junior developers is rather stable, but it rises gradually after around 5 years of experience. It's conceivable that this is due to the fact that C++ is a difficult language to grasp. Learning takes years, but once you've mastered it, you'll be rewarded handsomely.

C++ developers are in high demand in the employment market, so understanding what to anticipate in terms of pay is crucial. C++, on the other hand, is extensively utilized in a variety of sectors, mostly in the application area. C++ is a programming language that is widely used. Microsoft Windows, Mac OSX, and Linux are all C++ and C-based operating systems, as are two of the most popular databases, MySQL and Postgres. C++ is also commonly used as a backend technology in graphics applications that involve computer vision and high-end graphical processing, such as video games. C++ is also appropriate for embedded systems (such as smartwatches and medical equipment), financial systems, telephone switches, cloud storage systems, browsers, and compilers. What makes C++ such a popular and well-known backend technology? It's an improved version of C that's general-purpose, compiled, statically typed, case sensitive, and free-form programming language. The STL in C++ provides extensive library support (STL). C++ is quicker than other programming languages, which is one of the language's greatest advantages. C++ developers are in charge of developing or altering efficient C++ code in order to create a variety of apps and programs. They're also in charge of dealing with memory problems. In other words, a C++ developer's job is to design executable programs that help organizations run more smoothly.

Other elements that contribute to a C++ developer's income: C++ has the advantage of being compatible with a wide range of technologies, both software and hardware. As a result, greater pay is paid to C++ engineers with extra abilities. The following are some of the top complimentary skills: experience with Android, OS X, iOS, Windows, and Linux, as well as databases (such as MySQL or MongoDB), memory management, TCP/IP protocol, continuous integration, and more, depending on the project.

Depending on the project and organization, knowledge of project management techniques, expertise with algorithms and data structures, awareness of the software development lifecycle, and familiarity with other programming languages such as C, C#, Java, Python, and others are required.

C++ programmers are in great demand, which has a major impact on their typical wages, particularly among experienced and senior programmers. Furthermore, their skill set might be extensive, encompassing a thorough grasp of cutting-edge technologies, both software and hardware. One of the keys to success is drafting a clear and thorough job description and outlining the demands up front. Another is a thorough technical examination of individuals throughout the recruiting process. Hiring C++ engineers is a difficult endeavor, but employing the appropriate screening and online interview tools may make all the difference.

C++'S APPLICATIONS

- **C++ Games:** C++ is fast and near to the hardware. It can quickly handle resources, offer procedural programming over CPU-intensive tasks, and it is close to the hardware. It can handle the complexity of 3D games and has several networking levels. Because of these advantages, it is the preferred platform for creating gaming systems and game development suites.

- C++ can easily create most GUI-based and desktop apps since it offers all of the necessary capabilities. Adobe Photoshop, for example.

- **Database Management Software:** It's also utilized in the development of database management software. MySQL and Postgres, the two most popular databases, are developed in C++.

- **Operating Systems:** C++ is an appropriate programming language for building operating systems since it is tightly typed and quick. In addition, C++ includes a large set of system-level functions that aid in the development of low-level applications.

C++ has five different career paths:

1. **Digital Electronic Engineer:** In addition to understanding of electronics, the contemporary electronic engineer needs excellent programming skills. C and C++ are widely used languages for developing software for electrical devices. When seeking for job in this field, having knowledge of firmware control and other relevant abilities is a plus.

2. **Software Engineer who works in real time:** Embedded systems are designed to work in real time. C++ delivers the low-level horsepower needed to make electrical things operate once again. When working as a software engineer on these types of systems, C++ abilities are usually required.

3. **Multimedia Desktop Application Programming:** Multimedia programs on the desktop – music apps, graphic design apps, and so on – rely on C++'s performance. To assist construct these visually oriented apps, developers often use libraries, which are occasionally written in C++.

4. **Manager of Software Development:** Senior C++ programmers who continuously demonstrate project leadership, including mentoring younger workers, are on their way to becoming software development managers. While some people like the technical side of things, those with excellent business sense and communication abilities are well-suited for managerial positions. Consider getting a graduate degree, such as an MBA, to give your CV a boost before stepping into management.

5. **Engineer, DevOps:** Many organizations use DevOps to fuel their software engineering operations because they want to build software rapidly and efficiently. Developers with knowledge in C++ and other DevOps tools like Docker, Kubernetes, and Jenkins are in high demand. Senior software developers can follow this route to a fulfilling career.

If you want to learn how to code in C++, this book is a fantastic place to start. For a variety of factors, we believe Android will continue to cement its global market leadership.

In this book, we covered a wide range of C++ subjects. Let us now go through the contents of this text in order to review and reiterate the facts and information we learned about C++. We began Chapter 1 by discussing the fundamentals of C++ and how it has grown. What characteristics do compilers have, and what are the different types of compilers? Learn about the functions and features of C++, as well as how to set it up on your computer. In Chapter 2, we cover the fundamentals of C++ syntax, as well as how to compile and run programs. What are the fundamental terminology of C++, such as semicolons, blocks, and keywords, and comments. We also learn about various sorts of data and variables and how to use several examples to illustrate types. Furthermore, what are Constants and Modifiers and their many types, as well as storage class, operators, and the various types of Loop and Decision statements. What is a function in C++, and how do you declare one? What are arguments and what are Numbers, Arrays, Strings, and Pointers? Finally, using various words and examples, we learn how to take care of Files in C++.

In Chapter 3, we cover how to convert data between numeric and string types, the limits and other properties of numeric types, and how to create cooked and raw user-defined literals. We also learn how to develop a library of string helpers and what std::format is for formatting text. Chapter 4 will cover Defaulted and Deleted Functions, as well as Lambdas and Standard Algorithms, in this chapter. We also learn how to Write a Function Template with a Variable of Number of Arguments and how to Simplify Variadic Function Templates using Fold Expressions. Learn more about how to use the higher-order functions Map and Fold. In Chapter 5, we'll study what memory management is and why it's essential, as well as what memory management operators are and why they're helpful. Furthermore, we will learn what dynamic memory allocation is, how to allocate memory dynamically, and why memory management is essential. What are objects' new and delete operators? In addition, we will learn about memory objects and custom memory.

Furthermore, Chapter 6, we will learn about several types of processors, how to compile our basic source code in Visual Studio, and what preprocessor directives are in this chapter. Furthermore, we discover what enables if is and when it should be used. What are enable if Classes and what are the scenarios that they may be used for? How to use std::enable if and enable if to compile classes and functions on a conditional basis, as well as how to create a member function conditionally. Furthermore, what are attributes in C++, and what is the list of them? What is the difference between standard and non-standard qualities, and how can we tell the difference? Since C++11, the following has changed, as well as the distinctions between C++ and C# features.

In Chapter 7, we focus on what C++ coroutines are, what constraints they have, how to execute them, and what happens when one starts running. We also discover what Heap allocation and promises are. What is the best way for a coroutine to get its promise object within counter. We'll also go through the co_await(), co_yield, and co_return operators in this section. We also learn what generators are and the many generators and Coroutines and C++ for Effective Async.

C++'s development was nothing short of phenomenal, a wonderful breakthrough that solved a slew of problems that programmers had been grappling with for a long time. While this book serves as an excellent introduction for learning about the key principles involved in this behemoth, you should continue on your journey as a learner and developer to fully understand this beast. Best of luck!

Index

Printed in the United States
by Baker & Taylor Publisher Services